Artificial Intelligence and Machine Learning for Business

How modern companies approach AI and ML in their business and how AI and ML are changing their business strategy

Scott Chesterton

Table of Contents

Introduction

Many people still relate Artificial Intelligence (AI) with science fiction dystopias, but that tendency is slowly declining as AI expands and becomes commonplace in our daily lives.

Today, artificial intelligence is a common phrase that is used everywhere.

While acceptance of AI in the mainstream, society is a new spectacle, it is not a new idea. The new field of AI came into existence in 1956, but it took several years of work to establish substantial progress toward building an AI system and making it a reality.

When it comes to business, artificial intelligence has a wide range of application. In fact, many of us interact with artificial intelligence in one way or another daily. From the mundane to the breathtaking, AI is already changing every business process in all industries. As artificial intelligence technologies continue to develop, they are becoming necessary for a business that wants to sustain a competitive advantage.

This book will shed light on how artificial intelligence and machine learning are transforming the business sector. We shall start by exploring the basics of AI and machine learning before diving deep on the applications of AI and Machine learning. You will also learn how to implement AI in your enterprise. Keep reading to learn more.

Chapter 1: Getting Started

Ten years ago, if you said the phrase "artificial intelligence" in a boardroom, there's a high possibility you would have been laughed at. For many people, it would make them remember sci-fi machines and sentiment.

Today it is one of the most popular phrases in business and industry. AI technology is a critical lynchpin of much of the digital changes happening today as companies position themselves to take advantage of the ever-growing large size of data being produced and collected.

Well, how does this change happen? Partly is because of the Big Data revolution itself. The nature of data has resulted in extensive research into methods it can be processed, analyzed, and implemented. Machines being more suitable than humans to this work, the focus lies on training machines to perform this smartly.

This raises the interest in research in the academia-industry and other open source community which resides in the middle. It has led to various success and developments that are demonstrating their ability to generate huge change.

What is Artificial intelligence?

The idea of what describes AI has changed over time, but in the center, there has always been the concept of designing machines which can think like humans.

Human beings have shown that they can interpret the world around us and use the information we collect to implement change. If we want to create machines to assist us in doing this efficiently, then it is sensible to use ourselves as a blueprint.

AI then can be seen as awakening the potential for abstract, and creative thinking plus the ability to learn.

Research and development work in Artificial Intelligence is divided between two branches. One is called "applied AI" which applies the principles of activating human thought to implement one specific task. The other is labelled "generalized AI"-which tries to implement machine intelligence that can convert their hands to any responsibility, much like a human being.

Research conducted in applied, specialized AI is already providing success in fields of study from quantum physics where it is used to model and predict the behavior of systems.

In industry, it is applied in the financial world for uses that extend from fraud detection to enhancing customer service by predicting the services that customers may need. In manufacturing, it is used to control workforces, and production operations plus predicting faults before they happen, thus allowing predictive maintenance.

In the consumer sector, most of the technology we are applying in our daily lives is being driven by AI from smartphone assistants like Google's Google Assistant, and Apple's Siri Assistant to autonomous vehicles which many people think will come to surpass the manually driven cars within our lifetimes.

Generalized is AI far off to achieve a complete human brain activation since it would require a comprehensive understanding of the organ than we currently have, and more computing power than is now available to researchers. However, that may not last for long given the speed at which technology is changing. A new computer chip technology is known as "neuromorphic processors" is being developed to help run the brain-simulator code efficiently.

Key Developments in AI

All these developments have been realized because of the focus on imitating human thought processes. The field of research has been most successful in recent times is "machine learning." You will briefly learn about this. This field has become essential to contemporary AI that the phrases "artificial intelligence" and "machine learning" are sometimes used interchangeably.

But this an imprecise application of the language and the correct way to think of it is that machine learning demonstrates the current nature-of-the-art in the broader field of AI. The middle ground of machine learning is that instead of being taught to implement every step by step, machines if they can be instructed to think like us, can learn to work by classifying, observing, and learning from its mistakes, the same way we do.

Machine Learning Defined

One thing that both Google's self-driving car and Netflix's recommendation share is that they use machine learning to a certain level to execute repeatable decisions, implement particular tasks and independently adapt with minimal human interaction.

Machine learning can be defined as the science of making machines learn and behave similarly like humans while autonomously learning from real-world interactions and sets of training data that we feed them.

Machine learning isn't a new technology. The algorithm behind pattern recognition and machine learning application have been in existence for quite some time. But it is only now that machine learning models are beginning to connect with more complex data sets and learn from previous computations and predictions to generate important decisions and results. Develop a correct model, and you have an excellent opportunity to avoid unknown risks and select profitable opportunities across your business.

Machine Learning Tools in the Business Sector

Google, Microsoft, and Apple are some of the tech companies leading in the application of machine learning. Apple has already produced its Core ML API, which is meant to increase the speed of artificial intelligence on the iPhone. Microsoft has the Azure cloud services that include an Emotion API that can detect human emotions like anger, surprise, sadness, and disgust.

One thing that these tools share is that they are dynamic and can adapt to new rules, newly acquired information, and new environments. Right from recommendation engines to facial recognition, machine learning is the primary tool for companies that handle big data and make big decisions. In a situation where the business has to be ahead of the current threats, human error, and competition, this technology allows organizations to become agile and reactive than before.

Additionally, incorporating machine learning to improve processes and make data-driven decisions, companies should be able to control the security of their data more effectively and in ways that don't slow employees down. The solution is adequate data protection.

Machine learning supports the analysis of large data quantities. While it provides faster, and more accurate results to select profitable opportunities, it may also demand extra time and resources to train it well. Integrating machine learning with AI and cognitive technologies can make it more effective in executing large volumes of information.

Chapter 2: Why Use Machine Learning

Artificial Intelligence will transform our future more potent than any other type of innovation. The frequency of acceleration of AI is already surprising. Nowadays, there is a rapidly growing volume and variety of available data, computational processing that is cheaper and more affordable storage of data.

Machine learning and Artificial Intelligence have been around since the middle of the twentieth century but only started to become popular in the last few years. Why is that so, and why is machine learning meaningful.

As previously defined, machine learning is a field of computer science that provides the computer with the potential to learn. The main focus of machine learning is to generate algorithms that can be trained to execute a task.

It is closely connected to the field of computational statistics and mathematical optimization. It has numerous methods such as Semi-Supervised Learning, Supervised Learning, and Unsupervised Learning and Reinforcement Learning, which each contains there on algorithms and use cases.

Why Machine Learning Matters

Artificial intelligence is critical in the future. Anyone who doesn't understand it will soon be left behind. They will be surrounded by technology to the point where they may start to think it is magic.

The speed of acceleration is already shocking. In 2015, Google successfully trained a conversational agent that besides interacting with humans as a tech support helpdesk, but it could still discuss morality, respond to general fact-based questions, and express opinions.

In the same year, DeepMind builds an agent that outplayed human beings at 49 Atari games, receiving game score and pixels as inputs. In the following year, DeepMind obsoleted their success by generating a new state-of-the-art gameplay method known as A3C.

At the same time, AlphaGo defeated the best human players at Go-an outstanding achievement in a game led by humans for two decades after machines defeated chess. Many masters could not understand how it is possible for a tool to master the complete nuance and complexity of this ancient Chinese war game strategy.

To better understand machine learning uses, consider some of the situations where machine learning is applied. Some of these areas include cyber fraud detection, self-driving Google car, and online recommendation engines such as Facebook, Netflix displaying movies and shows you may like, and "more items to consider," and "identify something for yourself" on Amazon.

All these examples describe the vital role machine learning has started to perform in the current data-rich world. Machines can support filtering of critical information that can assist in significant developments. We are currently seeing how the following technology is presently being used in different industries.

With the constant change in the field, there has been a continuous rise in the application, the role of machine learning, and demands. Big data has become quite popular in the last few years, that is because of the rise in complexity of machine learning, which assists in analyzing big loads of data. Machine learning has further changed how data extraction happens, and the interpretation happens by applying automatic sets of generic methods that have substituted traditional techniques.

Chapter 3: Supervised Learning

How much money will we generate by spending more dollars on digital advertising? What may happen to the stock market tomorrow?

When it comes to problems in supervised learning, we begin with a data set that has training examples with marked labels. For instance, when you learn to categorize handwritten digits, a supervised learning algorithm will accept thousands of pictures of handwritten digits plus names holding the correct number each image represents. The algorithm will then learn the link between images and related figures, and use the learned relationship to categorize new photos that the machine hasn't seen before. This is how you can deposit a check by taking a picture using your phone.

To demonstrate how supervised learning works, let us review the challenge of predicting a yearly income based on the years of education a person has completed. Expressed formally, we would like to create a model that estimates the link f between the number of years of higher education X and related annual income Y.

$$Y = f(X) + \epsilon$$

Still, you can define a complex model by adding a few rules that explain the degree type, school tiers, and years of experience.

However, sometimes, this rule-based programming may fail to work correctly with complex data.

Supervised machine learning overcomes this challenge by letting the computer complete the work. By selecting the patterns in the data, the machine can create heuristics. The critical difference between this and human learning is that machine learning can operate on computer hardware and is best learned through statistics and computer science.

For supervised learning, the machine tries to learn the connections between income and education from square zero by executing labeled training data via a learning algorithm. This learned function can be used to approximate the income of people whose income Y is unknown, provided you have years of education X as the inputs. This means you can apply the model to the unlabeled test data to approximate Y.

The focus of supervised learning is to make accurate predictions of Y when supplied with new examples of X.

Two Functions of Supervised Learning: Classification and Regression

The regression will predict a continuous target variable Y. It will allow a person to approximate a value, such as human lifespan depending on the input data X.

In this case, the **target variable** describes the unknown variable we focus on predicting, and **continuous** means there are no gaps in the value that Y can take on. The weight and height of a person are constant values. On the other hand, discrete variables can only assume a finite number of benefits. For instance, the number of kids a person has is a separate variable.

Income prediction is a classic example of regression. The input data X is made up of all relevant information about persons in the data set that can be used to predict an income like years of education, years, job title, years of work experience, and many more. These properties are described as features, which can be numerical or categorical.

You may need a lot of training observations as possible connected to these features to the target output Y so that your model can learn the connection f between X and Y.

Data consists of test data and training data. The training data contains labels, but the test data doesn't come with tags. This means you cannot tell the value you are trying to predict. It is critical that your model can generalize to instances it hasn't come across before so that it can do well on the test data.

So how are models created that make accurate, and essential predictions in the real world? Well, this is achieved through supervised learning algorithms.

Now let us move to the exciting part: learning more about algorithms.

We will learn some of the methods to implement regression and classification, and demonstrate significant machine learning concepts throughout.

Linear Regression in Machine Learning

This is a simple model for regression problems where the target variable is a real value.

For example:

Let us begin with an example. Assume we have a dataset holding information about the location of the house and the price. Our task is to create a machine learning model which can predict the price. Here is a look of our dataset:

Area (sq.ft)	Price (1k$s)
3456	600
2089	395
1416	232

When we plot our data, we may create something that resembles this:

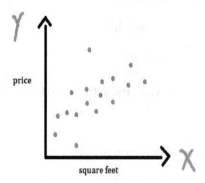

Let us dive deep into linear regression to comprehend this:

Linear regression belongs to the linear model. The model determines a relationship between input variables and the single output variable (y). They can be computed from the right mix of input variables (X).

If a single input variable is present, then it is called simple linear regression. However, multiple linear regression occurs when numerous variables are present.

Simple Linear Regression

This defines a link between the target variable, and the input variable using a regression line. Overall, a range is represented using this equation y = m * X + b. In this case, y is the dependent variable, X is the independent variable, m is the gradient, while b is the intercept.

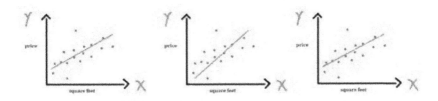

Multiple Linear Regression

The multiple linear regression equation can be applied when there is one input variable. But often you will handle datasets that have multiple input variables. A situation where there is more than one feature is called multiple linear regression, or linear regression. The previous simple linear regression can be summarized to multiple linear regression:

$$y(x) = w_0 + w_1x_1 + w_2x_2 + \ldots + w_nx_n$$

In the case of multiple linear regression, the prediction is a hyperplane in n-dimensional space. For instance, in the case of 3D, the plot will appear this way:

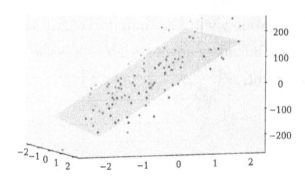

The cost functions

Different weight values provide different lines, and the task is to identify weights for which we attain the best fit. One thing that you want to find an answer is how you can determine the best line for your data. Or provided with two lines, how can you learn the best. For this, you need to create a cost function which measures, provided a value for the w's, how close is the y's to the corresponding true's. In this case, how does a specific set of weights predict the target value?

The mean squared error cost function is applied in linear regression. This is the mean over the different data points (xi, yi) of the squared error between the predicted value y(x) and the target value actual.

$$J(w) = \frac{1}{n} \sum_{i=1}^{n} (y(x^i) - y_{true}^i)^2$$

Residuals

The cost function describes a cost based on the distance between the exact target and predicted target, known as the residual. The residuals are defined as follows:

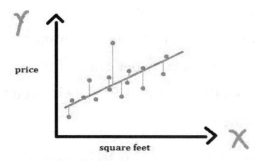

If a specific line is further from all the points, the residuals will be higher, and hence the cost function. In case a range is too close to the ends, the residuals will decrease, and thus the cost function.

Supervised Learning Use Cases in Data Science for Business

In recent years, machine learning (ML) has changed the way we run our business. A disruptive achievement that distinguishes machine learning from other techniques to automation is just a step from the rules-based programming. ML algorithms support engineers to leverage data without programming machines to adhere to a set of paths of problem-solving. But machines generate the correct answers depending on the data they receive. This ability makes business executives to reconsider the methods they use data to make decisions.

In layman language, machine learning is used to forecast on incoming data by applying historical data as a training example. For example, you may want to predict the lifetime value of a customer in an e-commerce store by determining the net profit of the future relationship with a customer. If you have historical data on various customer interactions with your website and net gains linked with these customers, you want to apply machine learning. It will support early detection of those customers who are likely to generate the net profit allowing you to concentrate more effort on them.

Although there are many learning techniques, the most common technique is supervised learning. In this section, you will learn about this field of data science and why it is low-hanging fruit for a business that plans to focus on the ML program, plus explaining the most popular use cases.

How Does the Supervised Machine Learning Operate?

Supervised machine learning requires that the expected solution to a problem is unknown for the incoming data but already is selected in a historical dataset. This means historical data have correct answers, and the role of the algorithm is to identify them in the new data.

For example, in a public dataset collected by a specific Portuguese banking institution during a 2012 marketing program, the bank focused on supporting its customers to subscribe to terms of deposits by making calls and pitching the service.

Typically, datasets are kept in tables that contain data items arranged in rows with variables in columns. The labeled data sets also include target variables, the values that need to be predicted in future data. In the following dataset, the target variable describes whether a customer has subscribed for terms of deposit after a call or not.

Unsupervised learning is used to identify defects in data that humans cannot assume themselves. It is more practical compared to reinforcement learning.

Use Cases of Supervised Learning

In 2016, Tech Emergence released results of a small survey among professional of Artificial Intelligence to describe low-hanging fruit applications in machine learning for small and large companies. Although 26 respondents could vote numerous times, they acknowledged that was evident already.

Interestingly is that groups used by Tech Emergence offered only a vague understanding of the distribution of use cases among various machine learning tasks. For instance, one can apply Big Data to any of the described groups because the algorithm can process massive and poorly structured datasets, no matter the industry and field of operation the data comes from. Additionally, sales tasks always intersect marketing ones when it comes to analytics.

age	job	marital	education	default	balance	housing	loan	contact	day	month	duration	campaign	pdays	previous	poutcome	target
30	unemployed	married	primary	no	1787	no	no	cellular	19	oct	79	1	-1	0	unknown	no
33	services	married	secondary	no	4789	yes	yes	cellular	11	may	220	1	339	4	failure	no
35	management	single	tertiary	no	1350	yes	no	cellular	16	apr	185	1	330	1	failure	no
30	management	married	tertiary	no	1476	yes	yes	unknown	3	jun	199	4	-1	0	unknown	no
59	blue-collar	married	secondary	no	0	yes	no	unknown	5	may	226	1	-1	0	unknown	no
35	management	single	tertiary	no	747	no	no	cellular	23	feb	141	2	176	3	failure	no
36	self-employed	married	tertiary	no	307	yes	no	cellular	14	may	341	1	330	2	other	no
39	technician	married	secondary	no	147	yes	no	cellular	6	may	151	2	-1	0	unknown	no
41	entrepreneur	married	tertiary	no	221	yes	no	unknown	14	may	57	2	-1	0	unknown	no
43	services	married	primary	no	-88	yes	yes	cellular	17	apr	313	1	147	2	failure	no
39	services	married	secondary	no	9374	yes	no	unknown	20	may	273	1	-1	0	unknown	no
43	admin.	married	secondary	no	264	yes	no	cellular	17	apr	113	2	-1	0	unknown	no
36	technician	married	tertiary	no	1109	no	no	cellular	13	aug	328	2	-1	0	unknown	no
20	student	single	secondary	no	502	no	no	cellular	30	apr	261	1	-1	0	unknown	yes
31	blue-collar	married	secondary	no	360	yes	yes	cellular	29	jan	89	1	241	1	failure	no
40	management	married	tertiary	no	194	no	yes	cellular	29	aug	189	2	-1	0	unknown	no
56	technician	married	secondary	no	4073	no	no	cellular	27	aug	239	5	-1	0	unknown	no
37	admin.	single	tertiary	no	2317	yes	no	cellular	20	apr	114	1	152	2	failure	no
25	blue-collar	single	primary	no	-221	yes	no	unknown	23	may	250	1	-1	0	unknown	no
31	services	married	secondary	no	132	no	no	cellular	7	jul	148	1	152	1	other	no
38	management	divorced	unknown	no	0	yes	no	cellular	18	nov	96	2	-1	0	unknown	no
42	management	divorced	tertiary	no	16	no	no	cellular	19	nov	140	3	-1	0	unknown	no
44	services	single	secondary	no	106	no	no	unknown	12	jun	109	2	-1	0	unknown	no
44	entrepreneur	married	secondary	no	93	no	no	cellular	7	jul	125	2	-1	0	unknown	no
26	housemaid	married	tertiary	no	543	no	no	cellular	30	jan	169	3	-1	0	unknown	no
41	management	married	tertiary	no	5883	no	no	cellular	20	nov	182	2	-1	0	unknown	no
55	blue-collar	married	primary	no	627	yes	no	unknown	5	may	247	1	-1	0	unknown	no
67	retired	married	unknown	no	696	no	no	telephone	17	aug	119	1	105	2	failure	no
56	self-employed	married	secondary	no	784	no	yes	cellular	30	jul	149	2	-1	0	unknown	no

Using ML to this dataset will assist determine the chances of other bank clients subscribing to terms deposit.

Training an ML algorithm means entering the above data into a machine using one of the mathematical approaches. The process supports the creation of a model that can define the target variable in future data. In this case, the role of an algorithm would be to categorize data items into two forms (yes/no). In general, supervised learning works with three major tasks:

Binary classification: The instance of binary classification is demonstrated above. The algorithm divides data into two sections.

Multiple classifications: In this approach, the algorithm selects between more than two types of responses for a target variable.

Regression: Regression models predict a constant value, while classification models focus on categorical ones. For example, predicting a net profit as a determinant of a customer lifetime value is a standard regression problem.

Challenges That Should Be Highlighted for Supervised Learning

Data Collection

Data is the central aspect of ML. The more data records you have, the better chance you have to create accurate models. You will learn more about data collection later on.

Labeling Data

In the previous example, labeling data doesn't appear like a hard task. If the data collection was carried out well, the labels were defined after the marketing call or after the campaign was over. But, typically, things are much complex than that.

Let us say you want to separate rotten apples from good ones automatically. And if you use image recognition methods, you will need to create a broad set of images comprising of rotten and good ones. Then you will need to place labels to them manually. Since image recognition can only work when you have thousands of examples, labeling may consume a lot of time.

In 2006, Google decided to crowdsource their image labeling by recommending to users a game-like experience that allowed them to label images hence contribute to the company's AI-development. Amazon also crowdsourced their labeling tasks through the development of a mechanical Turk platform where people can make money by allocating data labels.

Marketing and Sales

Digital marketing and online-driven sales are the major application fields that you may consider when you think of adopting machine learning. People interact with the web and leave a specific footprint to be reviewed. While there are substantive results in unsupervised learning techniques for marketing and sales, the most significant value impact falls in the supervised learning field.

Human Resource Allocation

The historical data from HR software, holidays, and vacations can be used to make expansive predictions concerning the workforce. Several automotive companies are learning from the patterns of unscheduled absences to predict the period when people may spend a day off and retain more workforce.

Time-series market prediction

This is an essential branch of machine learning, and statistics describe the time-dependent events. These can be cyclic changes in any market figures. Overall, time-series prediction takes into consideration time-dependent changes as seasons or holidays.

Today, time-series data can be applied both internal to ensure better planning features and for customer-facing applications. For example, eCommerce websites may be interested in monitoring time-series data linked to Black Friday to create discount campaigns better and make more sales.

Security

Most of the cyber-security methods revolve around unsupervised learning, especially the techniques that focus on anomaly detection. Discovering data items that may cause a threat. But there are different use cases where supervised learning is applied.

Filtering of spams: In 2017, 56.87 percent of all emails were spam. The abundance of spam examples supports both textual and metadata to filter this form of correspondence.

Malicious emails and connections: To detect malicious attacks is essential for all IT offices in organizations. Nowadays, different types of public datasets offer labeled records of malware that can be directly applied to create classifying models to secure your organization.

Asset Management and IoT

Digitalization goes past internal IT infrastructure. As corporate assets continue to become smart using the Internet-of-Things, different smart sensors can collect and stream asset data directly to public clouds where it can be centralized and further applied in resource management and supply chain enhancement.

Logistics: Finding solutions to logistics cases is a dynamic task because managers need to account for the delivery time, whether focus, budget, and driver's features, and other changing data.

Since supply chain management is a big challenge for many businesses that have real datasets and assets, then creating AI-backed recommendation systems is a great opportunity that can be adapted easily.

Prediction of outage: Another great opportunity is to make use of the history of machinery outages to predict early failures. Complicated ML algorithms can predict based on apparent factors that humans may not know. This makes it possible to support the maintenance of lower cost. And this method suits industries where asset management has been highly controlled.

Entertainment

Another use case field for machine learning is entertainment. In this field, users interact with algorithms directly. These can drive the gamut from face recognition and various visual alterations. This sector belongs to AI startups that plan acquisition and software shipping that can be embedded in different market products.

Jumpstarting machine Learning involves data

The most approachable industry for supervised learning is those that produce the most data, which can be organized and centralized inside a company. In case the data sets have been already labeled, this makes it easy to adopt.

As the business continues to become digital, the data they gather may become more ML-friendly. This means paper ledgers and spreadsheets used in offices disappear for good, while CRM and different tracking systems reach the plateau of standard practice.

So the first thing to jumpstart the machine learning program is to examine the data and consider a classification plan and terms of regression to describe the type of responses you can acquire.

Chapter 4: Unsupervised learning

Unlike supervised learning, when it comes to unsupervised learning, the dataset doesn't have a label. What you will perhaps learn, when there are no labels, is how to reconstruct the input data using a representation. Given the low percent of labeled data around the world, the notion that supervised learning cannot be used in most data, and the fact that models can learn best when more data is trained, the opportunity for unsupervised learning on datasets without labels is massive. The future of AI, in large part, relies on unsupervised learning become better and better.

The properties acquired by deep neural networks can be applied in clustering, regression, and classification. Neural nets are typically universal approximators applying non-linearities. They generate "good" properties by learning to compile data via pretraining. In the latter case, neural nets get into arbitrary loss functions to integrate inputs to outputs.

The properties learned by neural networks can be directed into other types of algorithms, including traditional machine-learning algorithms that combine input, logistic regression that classifies it, or simple regression that predicts a value.

So, you can consider neural networks as an aspect that regularly combines into other functions. For instance, you can create a convolutional neural network to learn the image properties on

ImageNet using supervised training, and then you could pick the features learned through a neural network and transfer them into a second algorithm that would learn to group images.

Here are properties of use cases build using neural networks

K-means Clustering

This algorithm is used to automatically label stimulations depending on their raw distances from other input in a vector space. There is no loss or target function; k-means has centroids. It builds centroids using repeated averaging of all the data points. K-means defines new data by proximity to a certain centroid. Each centroid is connected to a label. This is an excellent example of unsupervised learning.

The primary function of clustering is to generate data points groups.

Steps of K-Means Clustering

1. Definition of the k centroids. These will be initialized at random. They are also better algorithms for initializing the centroids that create more convenience.

2. Find the nearest centroid and update the cluster assignments. Allocate each data point to every k clusters. Every data point is allocated to the closest centroid's group. In this case, the measure of "nearness" is a hyperparameter.

3. Transfer the centroids to the center of their clusters. The new position of every centroid is computed as the average position of all data points within the group.

Continue repeating steps 2 and three until when the centroid stop is moving at every iteration.

That is a brief description of how k-means clustering operates.

A real-life application of k-means clustering is defining handwritten digits.

Hierarchical Clustering

Hierarchical clustering resembles regular clustering, except that you focus on creating a hierarchy of clusters. This can be important when you need flexibility in the number of groups you want. For example, think of arranging items on an online marketplace like Amazon. On the homepage, you may need specific broad categories of items for easy navigation, but as you get specific, you will want to increase the levels of granularity.

In the case of outputs from an algorithm, the cluster assignments also create a great tree that notifies you about the hierarchies between the clusters. Next, you can select the number of groups you require from this tree.

Steps for hierarchical clustering

1. Begin with N clusters, one belonging to each data point.

2. Integrate two clusters close to each other. Now you will have N-1 groups.

3. Recalculate the distances between the clusters. There are different ways to achieve this. One of them is the average linkage clustering. In this approach, you need to consider the distance between two clusters as the average distance between all the respective numbers.

4. Repeat steps 2 and three until you find a single cluster of N data points. You see a tree as the dendrogram.

5. Select different clusters and draw a horizontal line inside the dendrogram. In this example, if you want k=2 groups, you need to bring a horizontal line around a certain distance.

The curious pupil in unsupervised learning

For several decades, machine learning has attained massive progress in different sectors. These successes have highly been achieved through deep neural networks. Both approaches require a training signal to be developed by a human and transferred to the computer. Therefore, the limits of learning are regulated by human trainers.

While some scientists think comprehensive training is enough to give rise to general intelligence, some believe that real knowledge will demand more independent learning approaches.

Take, for instance, how a toddler learns, her grandmother may sit with her and show her cars, or reward her with a gift for completing a puzzle. However, most of the toddler's time is spent exploring the world, trying to understand her surrounding, play, and make observations.

Unsupervised learning is an approach developed to build autonomous intelligence by gifting agents with rewards for learning something about the data they observe without a specific task in mind. This means the agent learns for learning.

An excellent motivation for unsupervised learning is that, although the data transferred to the learning algorithms are rich in internal structure, the targets and rewards applied in training are generally sparse. This means that a massive percentage of what is learned by an algorithm must include understanding the data itself instead of using the knowledge to a specific task.

Learning by Creating

Probably, the most straightforward goal for unsupervised learning is to train an algorithm to produce its own data instance. These are referred to as generative models, not only reproduce the data prepared, but create a model of the class from which the data was extracted. The guiding rule of generative models can create a convincing data example.

For images, the best generative model has been the Generative Adversarial Network (GAN) where two networks-a generators and discriminator take part in a contest of discernment.

The generator releases images to challenge the discriminator to believe they are real. Meanwhile, the discriminator receives a reward for detecting the fakes.

The reproduced images, random and messy, are enhanced over numerous iterations, and the ongoing dynamic between the network results to ever-more realistic images that are, in most cases, indistinguishable from real photographs. Generative adversarial networks can also produce details of landscapes determined by rough sketches of users.

Developing by Predicting

It is a notable family inside unsupervised learning. Here data is divided into a sequence of tiny parts, each of which is anticipated in turn. These models can be used to produce data successively by guessing what will arrive next, entering the guess as input and making a guess. Language models where every word is predicted from words before it is the best-known example. These models run the text predictions that appear on some messaging apps and email. A recent development in language modeling has allowed the production of plausible passages.

An exciting inconsistency within the text is that unicorns are considered as "four-horned," it is essential to probe the problems of the network's understanding.

By regulating the input sequence used to control the predictions, autoregressive models can be used to change one course into another.

Autoregressive models learn about data by trying to predict each piece of it in a specific order. A general class of unsupervised learning algorithms can be created by predicting any section of the data. This may involve excluding a word from a sequence, and trying to predict it from the remainder.

By learning how to create localized predictions, the system is forced to learn the whole data. A significant worry about generative models is the ability for misuse. Altering video and photo evidence has been achievable for a long time; generative models could make it easier to edit media with malicious reasons.

Re-imagining intelligence

Generative models are essential in their ways. Waiting for an agent with the potential to produce data is a means of imagination, and thus the possibility to plan and reason about the future. Even without explicit generation, the studies indicate that learning to predict various features of the environment enhances the agent's world model, and thus raises the ability to find solutions to problems.

These results synchronize with our intuitions about the human mind. The potential to learn about the world without explicit guidance is the reason for what we refer to as intelligence.

Implementing supervised and unsupervised learning in your business

Machine learning can be an excellent tool for creating actionable business insights from big data. However, machine learning algorithms differ in the way they apply data to learn, with critical implications for business applications. Learning how supervised and unsupervised techniques work and the differences between them is important to automate your business.

Supervised learning

Supervised machine learning expects data scientists to train the algorithm to generate the correct result for a particular input dataset. Typically, this requires feeding the algorithm with massive data, along with the conclusions that the machine needs to extract from the data.

With sufficient training data, the machine learning algorithm should develop the correct conclusions when transformed to lose on new data.

This is a unique algorithm when it comes to business with the bandwidth to train the algorithm because it can be used to complete tasks from error-correcting financial audits to automate unstructured data entry.

Supervised machine learning algorithms can be applied as cognitive automation to support image recognition and draw information from unstructured data.

The drawback to supervised learning is that it extracts data. Most importantly, that data should be manually curated by human beings before training the algorithm.

Data has to be labeled based on a defined set of input variables and classified into a limited set of output possibilities. While more training data will result in an accurate algorithm, this process demands additional labor and depends heavily on having a stockpile of historical data.

Unsupervised learning

Unsupervised learning is much more complicated than supervised learning, but it creates doors for a particular set of applications. Unsupervised learning doesn't have a training phase. However, the algorithm is provided with a dataset and uses the variables inside the data to select and separate natural clusters.

The benefit of the following algorithm is that it doesn't need the same labor-intensive data curation that supervised learning demands. Secondly, unsupervised learning can detect patterns that cannot be seen by humans because of the human biases during analysis.

A significant application of unsupervised learning is customer segmentation. In this example, the algorithm is naturally blind to underlying biases in the way the company may focus on its customer demographics. The result is that unsupervised learning can generate a particular set of customer segments, with inferences for marketing practices.

In conclusion

Data scientists use different types of machine learning algorithms to identify patterns in big data that result in actionable insights.

Supervised machine learning is popularly used between the two. It includes algorithms like linear and logistic regression, and enable vector machines. Supervised learning is named so because of data scientist performs the role of a guide to train the algorithm what conclusions it should develop.

Supervised learning requires that the expected output of the algorithm is known plus the data used to list the correct answers.

For instance, a classification algorithm will identify pictures of cars once it is fed with a dataset of images that have been labeled with the names of vehicles and some features of identification.

On the flipside, unsupervised machine learning is focused on artificial intelligence. The concept that a computer can learn to detect complex processes and patterns without a human to guide.

While unsupervised learning is complicated for specific business use cases, it sets the path to solve challenges that humans would want to handle. Examples of unsupervised machine learning algorithm include k-means clustering.

Although a supervised classification algorithm depends on entered labeled images, the unsupervised algorithm will determine inherent similarities between the models and separate the groups accordingly.

Chapter 5: Building Machines to be More Like Us

The function of Artificial Intelligence in business has changed from initial sci-fi notions of movie robots and talking doors. In a world where human-machine interface technologies change at a terrific speed and one where talking doors are a more of a reality, the more imperfect and almost human the next developments of AI can be, the more "perfect" it becomes.

Now we can apply AI tools to decide whether social media outputs-Flickr images, tweets, Instagram posts are being produced by software bots programmed by malicious hackers or whether they were created by genuine humans. The critical thing here is that computers are still slightly too perfect when they complete any task that emulates human behavior.

Even when programmed to include common misspellings and the phrases of the local language, AI is still flawless. Humans are more interactive, more context-aware, more relaxed, and altogether imperfectly entertaining. Programming in sarcasm and traits of human personality are always a significant risk. It appears like medical developments like robots taking over risky tasks and automation of difficult tasks are some of the significant benefits that AI can bring to people of all types.

Martin Moran-director at InsideSales, a company that focuses on self-learning engine for sales acceleration highlights engineering, customer service, and administration as the areas set for AI growth.

"Essentially, it is the admin-heavy departments that stand to benefit most from AI today. We have taken AI out of the movies and reached the tangible 2.0 generation of cognitive intelligence," he says.

Moran believes that the next step of AI will emulate humans more closely and be developed on the ground of massive processing power, access to large amounts of data and highly complex algorithmic logic, similar to our brains. Similarly, the right and lasting effect on business will only occur if this AI intelligence is deeply rooted in the workflow process itself.

The state at which we can interplay the nuances of natural language understanding with human behavior trends in their right contextual environment pushes us to a higher level of AI machine control. The ability to develop AI using idiomatic peculiarities of actual people could make it possible to apply AI in real business workshops, offices, and factories. Well, how can we build machines to be more like us?

Operational Intelligence company Splunk says the right way to entirely change AI exists in the machines, and not in any study of humans in the first instance.

The foundation of machine learning lies in the insights that can be generated through analysis of humans using machines by the data left on those machines.

Every human interaction with a machine leaves a trace of machine data. Extracting this data provides us with an accurate record of our exact human behavior, from our activity on an online store to who we communicate with or where we travel through the geolocation setting on a device.

The majority of this type of data is only partially retained by most organizations, and some of it isn't traced at all. When we begin to digitize and locate the world around us to a more granular level, then we can start to develop more human-like AI that has a closer reflection of our behavior.

The central aspect that AI requires to focus on is where it fits more naturally into what we may refer to as the narrative of human interactions. AI intelligence has to be intrinsically embedded in the fabric of the way firms operate. Only then can the AI brain begin to learn about the imperfect world surrounding us. Humans require to adapt to a future where we need to interact with and work alongside computer brains every day.

A new report released by the Project Literacy campaign, overseen and convened by learning services company Pearson, predicts that the present speed of advancement in technology driven by AI technology will come to defeat the illiteracy level of more than one in twenty British adults in the next 8years.

Machine reading isn't mastering the complete nuances of the human language. But progress in technology means that it is likely machines will attain illiteracy potential surpassing those of 16 percent British people in the next decade. This is according to professor Brendan O'Connor of the University of Massachusetts Amherst.

What will happen next with AI is emotional? This means AI will manage to understand, categorize, and then act upon human emotions. Typically, this work has been straightforward. A picture of a person smiling and showing their teeth is probably happy. An individual with furrowed eyebrows may be angry or frustrated and so forth. Of late, we have begun to include additional contextual details about what the user may be doing, or where they may be situated, then a correct picture of mood and emotions is developed.

The natural language interaction company Artificial Solutions believes it is working on the next generation of AI cognizance. By building a world full of computer "conversations" that are a world from what we may consider being textbook English.

Artificial Solutions is working hard to develop AI that recognizes bad human habits and can acknowledge our unpredictable colloquial distinctions. AI today is at the point of becoming emotionally sensitive, believably naturalistic, and humanly imperfect. So be kind to your computer. It is about to get closer to you.

Chatbots Can Learn What You Want

The next change in customer service is powered by artificial intelligence so companies can start to focus on consumers with products based on their taste.

There was a time when it looked ridiculous to think artificial intelligence could be used to create a more human-like customer experience. Well, but that is what AI is being used today. AI examines a large amount of emotional and behavioral data in a move to communicate with us and generate brand experiences that are predictive and personalized.

When Unilever decides to incorporate AI in its operation in a move to increase the sale of Lipton tea, then you know times are changing.

AI is providing retailers with new strategies to ensure shopping is straightforward. The modern cognitive technology can understand, learn, reason, and interact the same way human beings do. This is a rapidly changing field.

IBM Watson, the company's cognitive computing service, was conducted by North Face-an outdoor clothing brand to drive their virtual shopping assistant. Artificial Intelligence supports shoppers to complete their online shopping by picking the correct jacks depending on their responses to questions linked to where they will use it, and when they will use it.

US department store chain Macy developed a shopping smartphone app driven by machine learning. This app allows customers to shop and ask questions like where a brand is found, and whether an item is out of stock.

AI will continue to be used to solve problems for customers instead of selling products. Advertisers can now spend effectively on their ads. Retailers can consider past behavior patterns, and personalize offers correctly.

We are living in times where cognitive technologies can be trained by the most experienced employees and this knowledge transferred to all staff and customers directly.

Various trends have powered recent developments. First, there has been a dramatic rise in the size of data associated with consumer behaviour. Secondly, computational power to support AI is more affordable. Thirdly, there is a big development in key AI techniques and machine learning algorithms.

When it comes to the organizational side, AI has caused a massive change in the way companies to look at the role of AI in building customer experiences. Although corporations thought that AI conflicted with the human design of experiences, they now acknowledge that it improves efforts.

Although many companies felt like AI interfered with human design experiences, now they see that it improves the experiences.

AI is doing well for subscription companies which sell and curate beauty products and clothes. Most e-commerce stores have applied AI to act as virtual personal shoppers to fill the gap left by shoppers who don't have time to shop.

There is no argument that AI has allowed companies to build a personalized experience that can predict what will embrace customers across the world.

For example, look-alike modelling where companies automatically detect the features of current customers and create an online platform for a lookalike collection of new prospects.

Application of similarity metrics makes it possible to micro-segment customers by detecting subtle patterns in behaviour that bind them.

AI has created a new playing field when it comes to the development of customer experience. If you have a powerful data and you can execute it with intelligence, smaller and savvy online customers can improve the grade too.

According to AI board level stuff Mr Singh, the current world is in an arms race and weapons n are adapting algorithms. The algorithms, transparency, and application will shape the competitive landscape.

The next phase of AI is concerned with personalization, where brands want to merchandise products depending on personal preference.

Retailers have been discussing personalization for years, but it has been an inspiration. So far, anyone with the potential to execute AI at scale, it is possible. Paradoxically, AI can customize experiences without the need to know personal information at all, but just by looking at online behavioural trends.

Computers conversing with humans

The chief strategy officer of Artificial Solutions Andy Peart says that through the application of Teneo Analytics Suite, computer brains are being trained to create sentences together to understand and successfully follow human conversation interaction.

Nowadays, computers have become smarter. What is important now based on the way computers react with us, complete speech, and display features of artificial intelligence is not simple as machines having the ability to "hear" us or react to our commands.

Now we want computers to understand us and create a degree of contextual awareness associated to what we are talking about. It is like we need to have "conversations" with other devices.

Why is computer speech recognition a bit thin in the first place?

Human languages are filled with colloquial terms, changeable dialects and a different accent. Then there is the problem with homonyms-words said the same way but with different meanings, so it is hard for a machine to differentiate between site, cite and sight. For example, cricket is an insect, and also a game.

Why does it seem hard to give computers a conversational power?

As smart as it is, plain old automated speech identification technology has begun to be commoditized and, in some cases, made free. What is happening is breaking sentences up into blocks and offering contextual conversation memory. For instance, a virtual assistant can send a single request to the user's previous comment or question.

When computers started speaking to us, it was based on a simple children's language. Some of the voices were designed for children. My Speak & Spell was a box with a handle and a small green screen that tested skills in a grating tone.

But for adults, the clunky computerized voices of the 1980s, '90s, and early laughs were from real. When the train's voice said that the next stop was Port Chester using two phrases instead of Dorchester, then you knew that was a machine. It could not tell that New Yorkers pronounced the word as one instead of two. Put simply, a voice that sounded like a human was a person, and a voice that sounded like a machine was a machine.

This was okay when all we wanted were basic announcements with short phrases. However, if a fire erupts in a train, we all want to hear a human voice addressing us-and not just it would relax our nerves. It is because automated voices are very hard for us to understand for anything longer than a shorter sentence. We have adapted to interpret nonverbal voice cues while we listen to our fellow humans, and we get lost when they are missing.

If we want to replace assistants with Google Assistant, or we want an actual conversation with Alexa for the future, it has to speak like a human. Responding to verbal cues and sticking to the rhythm, music, and freewheeling flow of human conversation. To be truly important to us, we require computers to behave like humans. And that is really difficult.

What makes it hard? Prosody. That is the tone, intonation, stress, and rhythm that provides our voices with their special stamp. It is not the words we speak-it is the way we say the words. The great secret to the human voice is the melodies. Beyond the actual words we use, there is a lot that is going on that is difficult to teach a computer all of it.

What we hear currently are enhanced human voices, selected for us by the people who created them.

Intonation is a mix of four qualities: tone, intensity, speech, and loudness. A person can perform multiple combinations of these qualities while speaking, but Siri cannot.

There is always a limitation to what a machine can do. For instance, it can only speak what was fed, and each of us is special in different ways. When you are feeling happy, you have different means to reveal your happiness in your voice. The drawback is that we cannot feed that into a computer. This is a tough problem for engineers: algorithms have a limitation, but the human voice is not limited.

Some tech companies have solved this problem by picking a human voice with many personalities to include in their A.I- which then combines them to create speech.

So what you hear now and in the coming years are transformed human voices, selected for us by the people who build them.

As the voices improve, it is vital for the system not to trick you. You require a signal to the listener that it's a robot.

We are still in that period before fake voices start to compete with the real voice. Even with the various complications that exist, experts believe that we are left with a few advancements and computers will converse with humans. Reaching that point will solve various technological problems but will generate as many legal and ethical ones.

So, can artificial solutions make computer conversations more human-like?

It is not just a matter of them being human-like, although we have to build a new level of informal realism that is tangible and can even be chatty if you want.

Interactions like human memory power, and one that features "meta-level" awareness of the entire world, as long as the awareness is extracted from the internet. The free-format unstructured content in most of the human conversations makes it difficult for computers to establish the true intent of a user.

Chapter 6: Visualizing the Predictive Model's Analytical Results

Typically, you need to display the results of your predictive analytics to those who are essential. Below are some methods to apply visualization techniques to present the results of your models to the stakeholders.

Visualizing Hidden Groupings Within Your Data

Data clustering refers to the process of unearthing hidden groups of connected items inside your data. Most of the time, a cluster is made up of data objects of the same type as social network users, emails, and text documents. One way you can view the results of a data-clustering model is demonstrated in the graph. The graph represents clusters that were found in data gathered from social network users.

The data linked to customers were gathered in a tabular format, and then a clustering algorithm was applied to the data, and the three clusters were found: wandering customers, loyal customers, and discount customers. Imagine that the X and Y axis represent two principal components produced from the original data. Principal component analysis refers to a data reduction technique.

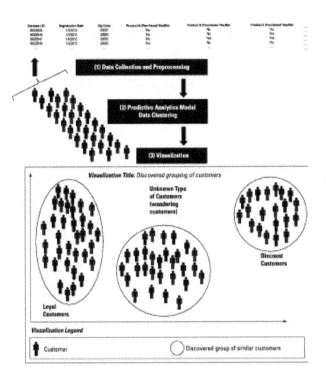

In this case, the connections between the three groups already describe where improved and targeted marketing efforts may perform most of the good.

Visualizing Data Classification Results

A classification model often assigns the specific class to a new data point it examines. The individual courses can include groups developed from clustering work.

Once you apply a clustering algorithm and identify groups in a customer data, you enter into a moment of reality: you get a new customer, and you want the model to describe the type of customer he or she will be.

The picture displays information on how a new customer detail is fed into the predictive analytics model, which then predicts the group of customers the new customer belongs to.

Customers A, B, and C are about to be assigned clusters based on the classification model. The application of a classification model results in a prediction where Customer A would belong to loyal customers, Customer B would be a wanderer, and Customer C would show up for the discount.

Determining Whether Your Machine Learning Model Has the Correct Performance

Once you create a machine learning model for your predictive modeling problem, how can you tell whether the performance of the model is good?

This is a commonly asked question beginners face.

Beginners always search for a solution to this question. You want someone to tell you whether the accuracy of x% or an error score of x is good or not.

In this section, you will learn the answer to this question and know whether your model is good or not.

Model skill is relative

Your predictive modeling task is special.

This consists of individual data, the tools you are applying, and the skill you will attain.

Your predictive modeling challenge hasn't been solved before. In other words, you cannot tell how a good model appears, or the kind of skill it may have.

You may have clues of what a skillful model appears as depending on the knowledge of the domain, but you aren't sure where the skill scores are attainable.

The best thing you can do is to compare the operation of machine learning models on your data to other models trained on the same data.

The baseline model skill

Since the performance of machine learning is relative, it is important to build a strong baseline. A baseline is straightforward and easy to follow the procedure for generating a prediction on the predictive modeling task. The skill of this particular model presents the foundation for the least acceptable performance of a machine learning model on your dataset.

The results generated from a baseline model displays the point from which the skill of all other models trained on the data can be achieved.

Examples of baseline models include:

- Predict the mean outcome result for a regression challenge.

- Predict the mode result value for a classification task.

- Predict the input as the output.

The baseline performance on your task can be used as the yardstick by which other models can be evaluated.

If a model attains a result below the baseline, something is wrong, or the model is not right for your problem.

What is the best score?

If you are dealing with a classification problem, the best score is always 100% accuracy.

But if you are dealing with a regression problem, the correct score is 0.0 error.

These scores are hard to achieve. All predictive modeling tasks have a prediction error. The error originates from various sources like:

- Noise in the data

- the incompleteness of the data sample

- Stochastic property of the modeling algorithm

You cannot attain the best score, but it is important to understand the best possible performance depends on your selected measure. You understand that actual model results will include a range between the baseline and the best possible outcome.

However, you need to look at the space of potential models on your dataset and identify what good and bad scores appear.

Identify the Limits of Model Skill

Once you select the baseline, you can decide to look at the extent of model performance on a predictive model challenge.

To identify a model that you can showcase works well in determining predictions on your specific dataset.

There are many approaches to this challenge. Two ways that you may want to try out include:

- Start High: Pick a machine learning method that is complex and known to work well on different predictive model problems like gradient boosting. Review the model on your problem and apply the result as a benchmark, look for the simplest model that realizes the same performance.

- Exhaustive Search: Review all the machine learning approaches that you imagine on the problem, and choose the method that attains the correct performance about the baseline.

The "Start High" approach is fast and can allow you to choose the boundaries of the model skill to expect on the challenge and identify a simple model that can attain the same results. It can still allow you to determine whether the problem is predictable fast, which is important because not all tasks are predictable.

The "Exhaustive Search" is slow and meant for long-running projects where a model skill is critical than any other concern.

Both methods will generate a population model performance score that you can compare to the baseline.

Why should you be sensitive when applying a predictive model to score new datasets?

The creation of a predictive model is a complex procedure, which involves different assumptions, challenges, and acknowledging the truth of what is being modeled. Models are not just created because a person is motivated to build one. A model is created from a well-defined theoretical conceptualization of the truth that is being modeled. Keeping that in mind, the modeler searches for the required datasets, which he knows can be used to create a model to predict results that are likely to attain whatever result that is being predicted.

Therefore, it is practically repetitive and irrelevant always to create models to predict the same results using "good" historical data of the reality that is being modeled. Once a model is created, it can be applied on new data tables with the same historical data and context used to create the model with knowledge of what is being predicted and what the historical nature of the new data appears like.

For instance, an auto insurance company creates a predictive model to address new customers who may want to enroll in their auto insurance policy, but need to score new customers to know the risks of using a range of variables. The insurance company requires to identify a score for every customer, which could be applied in the computation of their insurance cost and premium plus the risk that could be predicted and the associated liability.

A predictive model that is already created can be subjected to these new customers to calculate their predictive scores, which represent the level of risk. In determining the new dataset, it is critical that every variable applied in the model development is demonstrated in the new data table that is scored. Once the model is used on the new data table, a predictive score of the risks is calculated, and the score can be used by their system to determine the cost of insurance per year. The higher the score, the more unlikely you will generate a substantial effect to the insurance company in turns of the number of claims in a certain year. The lower your score, the more likely you will submit a claim. The scores can be arranged into decile.

That said, there could be a lot of things wrong with this technique. The assumptions applied both theoretically and in the application itself could result in negative results.

It is vital that you learn the historical context of the data that you want to model, or what you want to apply a model on.

A retail company may choose to build a predictive model to examine the type of catalog campaign features a higher performance. The historical nature of every campaign has to be understood clearly. As a result, building a model using historical circulation data of a certain catalog campaign and applying that model to score other campaigns may generate positive and negative results.

Predictive Modeling Techniques

Definition of predictive analytics

It is the use of statistical algorithms, and machine –learning techniques to compute the probability of future results depending on the historical data.

The focus is to go beyond descriptive statistics and demonstrate what has happened.

Predictive models have a known result and can be applied in building prediction results for new data. The results of modeling reflect the probability of the target variable.

A lot of companies are using predictive analytics to boost their operations and generate a competitive advantage using predictive analytics.

And the reason is that:

- It is faster and requires cheaper computers.

- Increasing volume and data type plus a lot of interest to generate important information.

- Harder economic status and a need for competitive differentiation.

Since the software has become more interactive and easy to use, predictive analytics isn't just a field of statisticians and mathematicians. Business professionals are also using these technologies.

Predictive modeling techniques have become the best tool in a marketing expert for enhancing the effect of campaigns and illustrate the return on investment.

With creative methods to improve data appears a focused, driven method to applying the correct content in front of the audience, at the right time. As long as teams access clean, and quality data, the ability to create campaigns to connect a target audience is better than ever.

This section will review some of the common predictive modeling approaches, with a major focus on three different types:

- Propensity models

- Intelligent recommendations

- Segmentation models

Within each category, you will identify five predictive modeling approaches your business can begin to implement immediately you have the tools in place to make it happen.

Segmentation models

The idea of customer segmentation has a long history in the marketing sector. What was once thought as an educated guess, has become a strategic approach fueled and assisted by hard data?

Below are predictive modeling approaches that help you to improve customer data to develop a refined audience for your campaigns.

1. Behavioral clustering

While leads convert customers, the path that directs them to conversion becomes valuable for a marketer concerned on leveraging predictive analytics.

That information, referred to as behavioral data, means fairly little alone. When integrated with demographic data, it inspires marketing teams to select commonalities and trends that build new target segments.

By pushing future leads that resemble the demographic background of that new target segment with the same series of behavioral actions, marketers can enhance conversions and correctly predict the effect of their campaigns.

2. Share of wallet estimation

This technique describes the percentage of a customer's budget that has been assigned toward your solution. The higher the percentage, the less likely that growth may occur through upselling or cross-sell opportunities.

When this technique is joined with product-based clustering, a correct share of wallet estimation indicates the amount of customer's budget is with competitors as well as the services or products you can sell to the customer to boost your wallet share percentage.

3. The likelihood of churn

Most marketers use predictive analytics purely for lead generation; this is wrong because the defensive abilities of strong predictive modeling are an exciting use cases.

Since it can be more expensive to get a new customer versus maintain a current customer, securing your current client-base should be the most important aspect across all industries.

You are determining a customer's ability to generate leverages of the same methodology created to classify possible leads by behavior. If you can correctly predict the chances of a lead converting a new customer, you can accurately determine the probability of the customer leaving.

Predictive modeling depends on quality data

None of this can take place without the presence of clean, quality data assisted by the best data management system. Quality data is the bedrock from which accurate predictive analytics depends on.

Chapter 7: Neural Networks and Deep Learning

What is Deep Learning?

Both deep learning and machine learning fall under artificial intelligence, but deep learning represents the next transformation of machine learning.

When it comes to machine learning, algorithms developed by human programmers are responsible for learning from data. They make decisions depending on what they have learned from data. Deep learning achieves that using an artificial neural network that acts similar to the human brain and enables the machine to analyze data in a format same as humans.

Deep learning machines don't need a human programmer to show them what to do with the available data.

Real World Examples of Deep Learning Models & AI

For many of us, concepts such as deep learning and AI are still unique. Most people who come across these terms for the first time respond with mixed feelings. How is it possible to make machines learn and implement job meant for humans? What defines a whole industry build upon making devices act like humans?

Although these questions are critical and demand discussion, it is easy to do away with a lot of skepticism. That means if we are ready to consider some real-world applications of deep learning and AI. This chapter will explore ways AI and deep learning are transforming industries.

Where Does Deep Learning Originate?

Both machine learning and deep learning are branches of AI. Deep learning is the advanced stage of ML. When it comes to ML, human programmers build algorithms that learn from data and perform analyses.

Deep learning differs from machine learning because it works on an artificial neural network which closely represents the brain of a human being. The same network enables machines to analyze data in the same way humans do. These machines with deep learning abilities do not need to implement the commands of human programmers.

Deep learning is realized through the vast amounts of data that we generate and use daily. Every deep learning model takes advantage of the data to support data processing.

Deep Learning Simplified

Artificial Intelligence is the most severe progress in human development. If you are reading this, probably you know concepts such as ML and deep learning.

So continue reading if you want to know more about how deep learning operates, and what is its position in AI and ML.

Deep learning is related to the emulation of human beings using the software.

Now that you know a lot about ML and AI. You may be asking these questions:

1. What is the function of deep learning in AI and machine learning?

2. How does deep learning operate?

1. What is the function of deep learning in AI and ML?

Both ML and deep learning belong to the same category of AI. Now, AI is a broad term. It is not something absolute.

In general, everything that we can do with machines and software that can emulate human intelligence is part of AI. It is found in certain technologies being used today.

Thus, in the following context, deep learning and machine learning are probably two methods, two methods to realize the condition of AI. But deep learning and machine learning are not independent of each other.

In other words, deep learning can include specific properties of machine learning, but the terms and application of machine learning do not require any properties.

Machine learning can be defined as a branch of AI where software programs can change their algorithms without the need for human involvement. Although traditional algorithms depend on input from engineers for changes in their functions, machine learning algorithms can manage to do so depending on the data used to train them.

Well, where does deep learning stands when compared with machine learning?

As said before, ML algorithms can change their algorithm to generate the right result. But an ML program has to be manually altered by an expert in case its predictions are inaccurate. However, the dataset used to train the ML algorithms have to be labeled and organized in a certain which allows the program to learn.

For instance, if you would like an ML program to learn to distinguish between images of dogs and cats, you need to feed the algorithm with different cat and dog images. However, it would only start to learn if you specifically label and organize the data in a means which supports the ML algorithm to master the differences between those animals' images.

Now you understand the challenges of ML, and the way an algorithm can alter its algorithm depending on the data fed isn't sufficient to activate human intelligence.

And this the point where deep learning comes in. Although ML attempts to activate human intelligence by mastering datasets and changing algorithms, deep learning strives to emulate the roles of the human brain itself.

Describing Deep Learning

Deep learning is a branch of ML. The link between deep learning and ML occurs because both have a role in AI. Additionally, both concepts work on the same principle. And that is changing algorithms without human involvement to generate the right result.

But unlike machine learning programming, deep learning network doesn't have to master the predicted outcome, but they can utilize unlabeled and unstructured raw data to generate the best results.

Alternatively, deep learning networks don't depend on a single layer of algorithms to generate results; these apply multiple layers of AI to process data and generate output.

What are artificial neural networks?

Artificial neural networks try to emulate the function of natural neural networks of the human brain. Therefore, to understand the way ANN operates, let us quickly learn how the neural networks inside our brains work.

Say, if I instruct you to choose a picture of a certain breed of dog among 10 different dog pictures, then you will need to look at each of the 10 pictures and ask yourself several questions to determine the breed of dog, and whether the breed is the one you are searching for.

In the process, there would be separate questions based on the query processed inside your brain's neural network. For example, what is the color of the dog? How large has it grown? Is the fur thick? The neural networks would analyze these questions in your brain in a split second.

In the same way, an artificial neural network(ANN) would have to analyze this case and accept the data through separate layers of a neural network. Each of the above layers would attempt to solve the challenge using its own set of concepts and queries. The final result would be the compilation of all the patterns that this neural network can identify within the data it was fed with.

Well, this is the way an artificial neural network operates in layman terms.

The next question to address is how does ANN fit in the definition of deep learning. Is ANN and deep learning the same thing?

Of course no, an ANN is not deep learning. However, we apply the term deep learning when pointing to a large number of ANNs.

For that reason, deep learning can still be considered as deep neural networks in certain cases. But no matter how you name it, there is no denying the fact that it plays a vital role in the AI implementation such as autonomous driving, and many others.

The best example of the abilities of the following neural networks was recently revealed to the world by NVIDIA with their study on a generative adversarial network, a form of ANN. These neural networks managed to define new and sensible faces by identifying patterns and learning through images send to the network.

Well, now you understand what deep learning is, but how can you use it in business.

For sure, these layman descriptions only serve to help with the basics of these concepts. Diving deeper into it would make it relevant to apply technical terms, which in general is irrelevant to those who are looking for business opportunities.

So here is what you need to know about using deep learning and neural network.

1. **More power**

Deep learning networks demand high computational resources, and most of its operations are GPU intensive.

2. **Large amounts of data**

Deep learning networks become what it is not just because of the development of its layers and algorithms, but mostly because of the way it learns. Data is the cornerstone of the above networks, the better the quality of data, the higher the information quality you draw out of these.

3. **Highly effective machine learning development companies and software development teams**

Not all companies require to invest in building deep learning algorithms by themselves. In fact, involving the best IT companies across the globe and having them as a partner is the most sought method for striking a competitive advantage through the application of technology.

Deep Learning Vs. Machine Learning

ML and deep learning have grabbed a lot of attention over the past two years. If you want to understand both of these terms in the most basic way, this section will help you.

So if you can stick with this part for some time, you will understand the real difference between deep learning and machine learning, and how you can leverage the two into exciting business opportunities.

So far, you are familiar with the basic description of the above terms.

This is a collection of cats and dogs' images. What do you think may happen when ML and deep learning networks may require to make some sense out of it?

Take a look at the above images. What you are seeing is a collection of cat and dogs' pictures. Now, say you want to select the images of dogs and cats separately using ML algorithms and deep learning networks.

Basics of deep learning and machine learning: When this task is solved using machine learning:

To help ML classify the images in the collection based on the two groups of dogs and cats, you will require to present it with the above images collectively. But how can the algorithm differentiate?

The answer to this question lies in the definition of ML, relying on structured data. What you will do is label the pictures of dogs and cats in a manner that will define certain properties of animals. This data will be sufficient for the machine learning algorithm to learn, and then it will continue to work based on the labels it learned, and categorize millions of other pictures of both animals it learned via the said labels.

When the Problem is Solved Using Deep Learning

Deep learning networks will use a different method to solve this same problem. The primary advantage of deep learning networks is that they do not really require structured data of the pictures to categorize the two animals. The ANN network using deep learning transfer input via different layers of the network, with each network hierarchically defining certain properties of images.]

In a way, this resembles how the human brain works to solve problems by sending queries through different hierarchies of ideas and related questions to identify the answer.

Once the data is processed through layers in deep neural networks, the system identifies the correct identifiers for categorizing animals from their images.

Note:

This was just an example to help you learn the difference in the way machine learning basics and deep learning networks operate. However, both deep learning and machine learning are not simultaneously suitable to most cases, including this example. The reason for this will be explained later.

Therefore, in this example, you have seen that machine learning algorithm demands structured data to learn the differences between images of dogs and cats, understand the classification and generate output.

On the flipside, a deep learning network was able to group images of both animals using data processed inside the network layers. It did not require labeled data, because it depended on the different outputs processed by every layer which compiled to create a unified means of classifying images.

Key points

1. The main difference between deep learning and ML emerges from the data presentation system. ML algorithms almost always need structured data, while deep learning networks depend on layers of the ANN.

2. Machine learning algorithms have been designed to learn to do things by relying on labeled data, then use it to generate other outputs with additional data sets. However, it requires to be protected from human intervention when the actual output isn't the one expected.

3. Deep learning networks don't demand human intervention because the nested layers in the neural networks subject data through hierarchies of separate concepts, which finally learns through their errors.

4. Data is the primary resource. The quality of the data determines the quality of the result.

What is not seen in the example, but is still essential to underline.

1. Because machine learning algorithms require structured data, they are not the best for solving complex tasks which involve a large amount of data.

2. While this example revealed the application of deep learning networks to solve a small task, the real application of deep neural networks is on a larger scale. In fact, going by the number of hierarchies, and concepts these network process, they are only suitable to compute advanced computations instead of simple ones.

3. Both of these branches of AI require data for it to generate any form of "intelligence." But what should be understood is that deep learning demands a lot of data than a traditional machine learning algorithm. The reason for this is that it can only highlight differences within layers of neural networks when exposed to million data points. On the other hand, ML algorithms can learn through pre-programmed defined criteria.

So with the above example and various explanation of deep learning and machine learning, you should now be able to tell the difference between deep learning and ML. Since these are layman descriptions, they do not involve a lot of technical terms which are most challenging to understand to those looking to using AI and ML for their businesses.

Below are nine applications of deep learning in different industries.

1. Computer vision

High-end gamers use deep learning modules frequently. Deep neural networks drive bleeding –edge object detection, image segmentation, and image restoration. So much so, they even drive the detection of handwritten digits on a computer system. Deep learning is running on a powerful neural network to support machines to repeat the mechanism of the human visual agency.

2. Sentiment-based news aggregation

News aggregators use deep learning modules to eliminate negative news and display only the positive things happening.

3. Automated translations

Automated translations did exist before the introduction of deep learning. But deep learning allows machines to perform better translations with the guaranteed accuracy that was missing in the past. Plus, deep learning is vital in translation extracted from images-something new that could not have been possible using traditional text-based interpretation.

4. Customer experience

Most businesses already apply machine learning to work to enhance the customer experience. Great examples include online-self-service networks. Also, many companies now rely on deep learning to build a reliable workflow. Many of us are already familiar with the application of chatbots by organizations. As the use of deep learning continues to grow, we can expect to witness changes in this sector.

5. Coloring illustrations

At a certain point, including colors to black and white videos used to consume a lot of time in media production. But deep learning models and AI introduced color to b/w photos and videos making the process simple. As you read, hundreds of black and white illustrations are being recreated in colored style.

6. Autonomous vehicles

The next time you are fortunate to see to an autonomous vehicle driving down, know that there are different models of AI working simultaneously. Although certain models highlight pedestrians, others are familiar at street signs. A single car can be trained by millions of AI models while moving down the road. Many have considered AI-driven cars as safer than human.

7. Language selection

This attempts to determine whether deep learning can distinguish dialects. For instance, machine learning will decide whether a person is speaking in English. It will then determine the difference as per the dialect. Once the dialect has been chosen, additional processing will be dealt with by a separate AI that focuses on a specific language. Not forgetting to say that there is no human invention in any of these steps.

8. Generation of text

Computers now can produce new text from scratch. They can learn the style of a text and highlight useful news pieces. AI focused text generation is fully equipped to deal with the complexity of opinion pieces on matters related to you and me. At the moment, text generation has made it possible to generate entries on just everything from scholarly topics to children rhymes.

9. Image analysis and generation of the caption

One of the best things about deep learning is the ability to detect images and produce intelligent captions. Also, the image caption done by AI is so accurate that most online publications are ready to take advantage of these techniques to save cost and time.

Chapter 8: Operationalizing AI and ML Projects by Companies

With a powerful technology that creates massive changes as ML, it can be hard to ignore the hyperbole. Sure, billions of dollars in investment are being invested in ML projects. Machine learning is the foundation of digital transformation methods. And to be sure, machine learning is what people talk about when they mention the general term "AI." So, it is essential to take time to review real-world ML capabilities being developed and used across different companies around the world.

Typically, the abilities of AI allow the computer to examine massive datasets to attain a "reasoned" conclusion regarding the subject being addressed, activating the human decision procedure, always with better decisions being generated.

Although it is simple to define AI and ML, the problem has been the application of AI daily. One field that has attained success is the content matching and suggestions for streaming media, radically changing the on-demand viewer experience. Instead of trying to limit the "expert" human work required to categorize, curate, and segment content into consumable forms, machine learning has become a critical tool in personalized content delivery. By reviewing user behavior, preferences, and most streaming services can accurately personalize recommendations and push the targeted content with a higher ability for monetization and interaction.

Overall, every industry should consider applying AI into their business models. You don't need to be a big company to use AI to get better services to your customers. AI can assist both small and mid-sized businesses, and complete customer product needs faster, transform the inventory systems by applying Just in Time processes, limit shipping, and stocking mistakes as well as facilitate the payment and collection procedure.

Business domains where AI is transforming the landscape

Life Sciences and Pharmaceuticals

Wherever you get into a death disruption argument, we can all acknowledge that aging is a challenging experience. Even if you don't look forward to immortality, you probably recognize that increased joint pain and susceptibility to illness and injury will destroy the quality of life a person.

However, deep learning can slow the aging process. Scientists now use technology to detect biomarkers associated with aging. Soon, a simple blood test could be sufficient to show the parts of your body displaying wear and tear, and your doctor could assist you to eliminate, and probably reverse the effects through lifestyle changes and medication.

Food

About 40 percent of a grocer's revenue is from sales of fresh produce. So, to assume that maintaining product quality is critical is like an understatement. But it is easy to say so than doing it. Grocers are at the whims of their supply chains and consumer uncertainty. Maintaining their shelves stocked and products fresh can be a dangerous balancing act.

However, growers have discovered that machine learning is the solution to smarter fresh food. They can feed ML programs with historical datasets and enter data about promotions and store hours as well, and apply the analysis to measure how much of every product to order and display. ML systems can as well gather information about public holidays, weather forecasts, and other contextual information. Then they release a recommended order after 24 hours so that the grocer has the right products in the correct measure in stock.

Businesses that apply machine learning in their workflows limit the out-of-stock rates by up to 80 percent, plus 9 percent in gross margin rise.

Media and Entertainment

Media companies can now make their content accessible thanks to machine learning. ML has made it possible for deaf Americans and those with hearing-impaired to watch and enjoy YouTube videos through the automatic captioning program.

Information Technology

Although machine learning generates multiple business insights, many organizations have failed to tap in AI technologies. But it has been predicted that there would be about 2.7 million data science jobs by 2020.

Law

Deep learning programs are critical in the legal industry. Legal phrasing can be hard to understand, but deep learning programs can analyze more than ten thousand documents.

There was a time when legal professionals tasked with the role to examine contract clauses that impact their client's business had to review stacks of documents manually. Now it is possible to feed them into a program that works faster and detect important terms for further review.

Insurance

Minimizing risk and underwriting is the goal of every individual, and that is why ML is an excellent tool in the insurance industry. Machine learning algorithms can use customer data and real-time data to determine the level of risk.

Also, the algorithms can customize rates based on the information, probably creating savings for insurance companies and consumers.

This process could be transformed using an in-depth analysis where ML programs gather unrelated social network data to create an accurate profile. The insurance industry can include artificial intelligence to define policyholders gainfully employed and who tend to be in good health.

Mostly, a person responsible for those parts of their lives will be a responsible driver too.

Education

Intelligent Tutoring Systems (ITS) has a massive ability in helping students learn. These AI programs work as virtual tutors and adapt their digital lessons depending on the strength of every child. Every time a student completes a quiz, an ML program analyzes the information to personalize future materials.

By "learning" the unique needs of a user and choosing the type of lessons most effective for them, the ITS ensures that student overcomes learning problems and retain a lot of knowledge. Research shows that students who apply intelligent tutoring systems do well on tests compared to peers who learn through group instruction.

Health care

Compared to other developed nations, the US spends a lot on health care per person than any other country. For example, the U.K spends less per person ($3,749) annually on health care than the United States. Despite the high spending, the United States doesn't have the best health outcomes.

The discovery of AI in decreasing the number of tests and making the right decisions on treatment promises to reduce the health care costs in the United States with more effective lifesaving results. As a result of the high expenses related to health care and the advantages generated by health care decisions, there is a likely chance of seeing exponential growth in the application of AI.

How AI and ML are Improving Customer Experience

What can machine learning and artificial intelligence do to enhance the customer experience?

AI and ML have already been intimately applied in online shopping. You cannot use Amazon or any other shopping service without receiving recommendations, which are typically personalized depending on the vendor's knowledge of your traits: browsing history, purchase history, and much more. Amazon and other online businesses would enjoy creating a digital version of the salesperson who knows you and your tastes and can guide you to products you will like.

Everything starts with quality data

To make this decision a reality, you need to begin with some heavy lifting on the back end. Who are your customers? Do you know them? All customers leave behind a data trace, but that data trace is a sequence of fragments, and it is challenging to associate those fragments to each other. If a customer has numerous accounts, can you detect?

If a customer has different accounts for business and personal use, can you connect them? And if a company uses various names, can you identify the single organization responsible for them? Customer experience begins with knowing exactly who your customers are and how they are connected. Removing your customer lists to avoid duplicates is referred to as entity resolution. It used to be the field of large organizations that could manage substantial data teams. Right now, we see the democratization of entity resolution. There are no startups that offer entity resolution software and services that are right for small to medium organizations.

Once you establish who your customers are, you need to find out how well you know them. Having a holistic view of customer's activities is key to mastering their needs. What data you have concerning them, and how do you apply it? ML and AI are being implemented as tools in the data collection process. When it comes to computing data streams that originate form apps, sponsors, and other sources, data collection can be intrusive and ethically questionable. As you continue to develop your customer knowledge, ensure you have their consent and that you aren't affecting their privacy.

ML isn't different from any other type of computing: the principle "garbage in, garbage out" still works. If you have low-quality training data, the results will be reduced. As the number of data sources increases, the number of possible data fields and variables changes, plus the possibility for error: typographic errors, transcription errors, and so forth. Traditionally, it could be possible to manually correct and repair data, but fixing data manually is an error-prone and tedious thing that disturbs most data scientists. For entity solution, data quality and data repair have been the topic of research, and a new set of machine learning tools for automating data cleaning are starting to appear.

When it comes to applications of ML and AI to customer experience, the standard field is in recommendation systems and personalization systems.

In recent years, hybrid recommender systems-applications that integrate multiple recommender strategies have become a lot common. Most hybrid recommenders depend on many numerous sources, and massive amounts of data and deep learning models belong to these systems. Although it is famous for recommendations to feature models that are only retrained periodically, advanced recommendation and personalization technologies will require to be in real time. Applying reinforcement learning, bandit algorithms, and online learning are starting to develop recommendation systems that frequently train models against live data.

Machine learning and AI are improving various enterprise tasks and workflows, plus customer interactions. We have seen Chatbots that automate different customer service. Currently, chatbots are more annoying than helpful. However, if it is well-designed, bots can result in excellent customer acquisition rates. However, we are just at the early stages of natural language processing and understanding, and in the last year, there have been different breakthroughs. As the ability to create complex language models changes, we will see Chatbots transform through various stages: from delivering notifications to controlling simple question and answer cases.

As chatbots change, we expect them to form an integral organ of customer service, not just an annoyance that you have to work through to get a human. And for chatbots to attain this performance level, they will require to include real-time recommendation and personalization. They will need to know customers as well as human.

Fraud detection is also another field that is incorporating machine learning. Fraud detection is trapped in a constant battle between the right people and criminals, and the stakes are rapidly increasing. Fraud artists are beginning sophisticated techniques for online crime. Fraud is no longer person-to-person: it is automated just like the bot that buys all tickets to events so that they can be resold by scalpers. As seen in recent elections, it is easy for hackers to gain entry to social media by building a bot that floods conversations with automated responses. It is difficult to identify those bots and block them in real time. That can only be done using machine learning, and still, it is a difficult task that can only be solved partially. However, solving it is an important part of re-building an online world where people feel safe and respected.

Development in speech technologies and emotion detection will reduce friction in automated customer interactions even more. Multi-modal models that integrate separate types of inputs will make it easier to respond to customers correctly. Customers may be able to reveal what they want or send a live video of a challenge they are experiencing.

Although interactions between robots and humans constantly place users in a creepy "uncanny valley," it is okay that future customers will be more comfortable with robots than we are now.

However, if we are going to look for customers using the uncanny valley, then we need to respect what they value. Al and Ml applications that impact customers will have to respect privacy; they will have to be secure and be fair and unbiased. None of these are simple, but technology will not increase customer experience in case customers end up feeling abused. The result could be more efficient, but that is a bad tradeoff.

What can machine learning and artificial intelligence perform for customer experience? It has already achieved a lot. But still there is a lot that it can make, and it has to implement in creating a frictionless customer experience of the future.

Chapter 9: Step-by-step Method to Develop AI and ML Projects For Business

The technology sector is in love with AI. Many different applications have been developed, ranging from automated customer service to high-end data science; this technology is famous across the businesses.

Artificial Intelligence is a prominent driving force in the technology sector. AI is the leading topic of discussion at conferences and revealing the possibility across different industries, including manufacturing and retail. New products are getting connected with virtual assistants, while Chatbots are responding to customer questions on everything.

At the same time, big corporate companies like Microsoft, Google, and Salesforce are embedding AI as an intelligence layer across their tech systems. Sure, AI is having its moment.

It is not AI that pop culture has made us expect; it is not the Skynet, or sentient robots, or even Tony Stark's Jarvis assistant. The AI plateau is taking place below the surface, making our current tech smarter and opening the power of all the data that enterprises gather. This means a broad development in machine learning, deep learning, and natural learning. These have simplified the process of incorporating an algorithm into a cloud platform.

For businesses, practical uses of AI can show up in different ways based on your organizational needs and the business intelligence insights extracted from the data you gather. Enterprises can incorporate AI from obtaining data to generating engagement in customer relationship management to maximizing logistics and efficiency in monitoring and maintaining assets.

ML is playing a huge function in the development of AI. Currently, AI is being powered by the recent changes in ML. There is no single success you can refer to, but the business value that we can mine from ML now is off the charts.

From the enterprise perspective, what is taking place now may affect some important business processes around control and coordination, as well as scheduling resources and reporting.

This section will describe tips from experts on the actions to take to include AI in the organization and to ensure that the implementation is successful.

1. Familiarize with AI

Find time to understand what modern AI can deliver. You can use TechCode Accelerator wide array of resources through its coordination with organizations like the University of Stanford. Still, you can turn to online resources and learn more about AI. There are remote courses offered by platforms such as audacity, and code academy. These can kick start your journey.

More online resources you can use to get started include:

- Microsoft's open-source Cognitive Toolkit

- Stanford University's online lectures.

- Google open-source software library.

- The link for the development of Artificial Intelligence.

2. Select the problems you need AI to solve

Once you are familiar with the basics, the next thing is to start exploring unique ideas. Think of how you can include AI capabilities to your current products and services. The most important thing is that your company should have in mind specific examples of AI applications to solve business challenges.

When working with a company, it is important, to begin with, a brief description of its major tech programs and challenges. You want to demonstrate how natural language processing, ML, and image recognition suit those products. The specifics change depending on the type of industry. For instance, if the company performs video surveillance, it can retain a lot of value by including ML to that procedure.

3. Prioritize important value

In this step, you analyze the financial cost of the business across different AI applications you have chosen. To prioritize well, you have to review the dimensions of feasibility. It should offer you a chance to prioritize and establish the value for the business. This step will also demand ownership and acknowledgment from top-level executives.

4. Accept the internal capability Gap

There is a difference between what you want to achieve and what a company can achieve in a specific time frame. That is why it is critical for a business to be aware of the limits from a tech perspective before diving into AI.

Sometimes, this can demand more time; however, by concentrating on your potential internal gap implies that you know what you want to achieve.

Depending on the available business, numerous projects or teams can help you to do this organically.

5. Look for professionals and prepare a pilot project

Once your business is good to go, next, you need to think of integrating AI. The secret with this step is to start small, set project goals, and keep in mind what you know and what you don't know about AI. This is the perfect moment to invite external experts.

For a first project, don't set a lot of time, even 2-3 months could be enough for a pilot project. Once the pilot project is over, you should figure out what the longer-term project will be and whether the value proposition is necessary for your business as well as people who are skilled in AI.

6. Start a team for integrating data

The first you need to do before you can apply ML into your business is to clean the available data. Corporate data is found in different data silos and could be in the hands of business groups with a different objective. For that reason, the correct step to ensure that you acquire useful data is to set up a team that will clean the data and removes any inconsistencies that may be present.

7. Implement small

When it comes to the implementation phase, you will require to do it in little bits instead of going big. Make small implementations, and try to read the feedback. From the feedback, you can improve slowly.

8. Have storage plans in your AI program

Once you shift from a small size of data, you will require to factor in the storage requirements to involve AI solution. Enhancing algorithms is a vital step towards attaining great results. However, without a large volume of data to assist develop accurate models, AI technologies cannot offer much to ensure you attain your computing needs.

Besides that, you need to improve AI storage for data workflow and modeling. Setting aside time to analyze your options can have a significant positive effect on how the system works once it is online.

9. Involve AI as part of your daily plans

AI provides addition automation and insight, and this is an excellent tool for workers to make AI become part of their daily routine instead of something that replaces it.

Corporate organizations should be open on the way tech operates to solves problems in a workflow. This will provide employees with a unique experience so that they can visualize the way AI optimizes their role.

10. Incorporate some balance

While creating an AI system, it demands you fulfill the needs of the tech and research project. The main thing you need to factor in before you begin to design an AI system is creating balance within the system. This may look obvious, but in most cases, AI technologies are built around specific features of how the team considers realizing its research goals, without mastering the requirements and limitations of the hardware and software that would augment the research.

For companies to realize this balance, they should ensure that they have enough bandwidth for storage, networking, and graphics processing.

Alternatively, you require to balance the way the general budget is used to fulfill research with the desire to safeguard against power failure and other means via redundancies.

How to Develop an AI Startup?

Right now, AI is a big thing. Everyone has a say, and this can be difficult to avoid the hype, and dive into practical down to Earth questions.

In this section, you will learn what AI is at a basic level, without getting confused by the extensive knowledge. Next, you will learn the four general steps you need to follow when you want to launch an AI business.

It is also important to note that the hype around AI can make you feel like if you are not using AI, you are going to be left behind. But in many forms, AI is still in the infant stage, and it is not always clear when it's the right time for you, and when it is over complicating matters.

That doesn't mean that you should avoid using AI if you are about to launch a new company. Many severe problems need to be solved, and AI technology as it is now can help.

AI at the Conceptual Level

You would be forgiven for failing to know how to perceive AI. Can it be a robot walking in your house or an app in your smartphone? Maybe it's the entire phone. Much of what has been documented about AI makes it difficult to fail to know what AI is. Plus, there are debates about AI vs. ML. In this section, we shall gloss over the differences, and focus on the broader topics, and how they apply to the problems entrepreneurs face.

Put, AI is a software piece that, like much other software, can accept input, and turn it into output.

The only significant difference from many other software types is that the program doesn't give it a step by step commands on how to perform a transformation, and may not even be aware what those steps are.]

Just like any other software, AI can be packaged in different ways; it could be incorporated within an app, a voice managed the device or a website.

To keep things simple, when we talk about AI, we will be referring to the software bit that accepts input and generates output. The critical thing is that it can shift from input to output in moments where it is difficult to write down explicit commands on how to get from input to output.

These are tasks that humans are traditionally good at and computers are historically bad at, at least individually. But in most cases, humans are worst at everything.

Common examples consist of identifying a photo, highlighting emotion from a sentence, and scanning medical test results by searching for subtitles but high deviations from the expected data.

Classifying AIs

You can divide AI into two types: one that performs common tasks in many different forms like converting spoken speech into written words, and one that deals with varying tasks like choosing whether a set of heartbeat data reflects on a heart problem. The difference is critical because the common challenges are already solved, and you can use an existing AI instead of building your own.

Existing AIs

There are several problems where AI is good at evaluating. For instance, face detection in photos or even speech recognition. Since these are common problems, most of the work has gone into developing AIs to solve them. This means you don't need to complete the hard part of these AIs; you can benefit from the work a person has already completed.

The big cloud offers various developed AI products for different tasks, which you can apply on a "pay as you use" model.

Alternatively, since these services are AI based, it is irrelevant if you are using them. All you need to care is that it provides you with the correct answers.

Before you can move forward to develop your own AI, determine if there is one already developed and packed in a manner that you can use.

Custom or Bespoke AIs

The next type of AI is custom built. This is the most interesting part. If you are attempting to complete a task that isn't common enough for current solutions to be readily present, you need to build your own.

At the abstract level, this is simple, but like other things, it gets difficult to dive into the detail.

A Brief Look into AI Details

There are several technical approaches, but the one that receives the highest focus is neural networks. A neural network refers to a complete collection of simulated neurons that are joined together. A signal is transferred to the first neurons that may or may not signal other neurons, and so forth. At the other end of the network, an output signal is generated. For instance, the output signal may comprise a list where the faces are located in a photo.

There are two methods of creating a neural network: building the web and training it. To build the net, you have to select the number of neurons there are and the type of connections between them.

Once you have developed a neural network, you need to train it. Training a system means configuring every node using a mathematical function that notifies it when to transfer a signal it gets, and when not to. Luckily, you cannot do this by hand; it is incredibly impractical.

To train a neural network, you use a training framework to supply your system with a large percent of training data. The training framework builds the math functions for each neuron.

The integration of size and connection of neurons, plus these functions is referred to as a model.

Once you have a model, there are several containers that you can load it in, and the standards exist that let you load your model in a web-based platform.

From an individual attempting to build AI to apply in a business context, the biggest challenge you will encounter is the type of data you need and where you can get it.

Recommendation for a person creating an AI-based startup

There are four important steps:

Determine your problem-solution fit

As with any startup, if you are not solving a problem that customers are ready to pay for, then you don't have a startup.

Before you make big steps, it is crucial to test and be sure that there are people ready to pay for what you want to create, and that is possible to establish what you have in mind.

You can test to see whether people are ready to cash in for your solution by implementing different solutions like a traditional lean technique. The most exciting thing about AI is that it is easy to build a simple version of your solution by involving real humans with a mix of various components.

In most cases, a mix of AI services, existing non-AI services and different humans completing major activities can develop a prototype that simulates your expected solution, allowing you to execute product solution tests before you commit to creating a complete AI.

This triggers the question; do you need to develop AI? Just because it is a solution to a problem, it may not be the only method to do so. Each case is unique, but at this point, when you are applying real humans to test your problem, stop and ask yourself this question: "What is it about my problem that means an AI is the best or even only solution?"

It is difficult, but still necessary to determine whether the AI you are going to depend on can be developed. Not every problem requires to build AI. This is something challenging to do on your own, but you can look for someone who can assist you in running tests with your data to determine whether it is possible.

A building game

If you have attained a level where you know your customers exist and you are confident your AI can be developed, it is time to move forward, establishing the first generation of your AI. As said before, you need to collect some data, curate it, and ensure it is important, next design a model and train it.

Practically, you need to be aware that in most cases, the task of searching for data, curating, and controlling the data is the most significant and hardest part of the problem. Training a model usually consumes most of the computer time, but it is collecting and understanding the data that still require human intelligence, and that is the point where you need to expect to spend most of your time.

Create your product

At this stage, you have a working AI, but it is not easy for your users to get tasks done. By now, you are probably okay with talking about trained models, but it is unlikely your users are.

Probably, they want to pick their phone and launch their app, or even access a website or talk to their voice-activated the home assistant.

This means you will need to package your AI into a product. Something that contains a user interface, and probably performs several things beyond just what AI does.

Keep in mind that a great product is one that creates solutions to a real-world problem. It is not good to have an AI program that can only look at a photo and tell you where the faces are. If your real-world problem is allowing people to learn names from a collection of photographs, you'd need to do a bit more.

For instance, you would want to package that AI in a product that discloses your user's original photo, with boxes near the faces, and maybe ask them to write out the name of each face in a text field. That way it can disclose to them a sequence of flash cards to recall the names of everyone they are going to encounter when they attend that wedding, their new data just requested them to meet them.

Develop ways for enhancing your AI

Training your AI with quality data makes it better. Once your startup is running, you will discover that you have a lot of data to work with. You will find that you are receiving a massive amount of data. You will have data that you initially didn't have when you began to train your AI.

As you collect a lot of data, you will want to retain your data for training purposes. So the things you need to factor in are how you will test the data in case the new generation is better than the old one.

In summary, this chapter was to give you a primer on AI so that you feel motivated to move forward with the idea you are thinking about. Moving forward may imply to begin testing out and building your own AI, or it may mean requesting whether you need to go down the AI pathway. If so, that is an excellent question to ask.

Whichever way, your next step is to have a conversation with your technical team. If you are yet to set up a professional team, you can get in touch with someone to get more information, and answers to your questions.

Having experience in creating projects, knowledge about data sets, and working with AI, you will be in an excellent position to help you with your questions.

Chapter 10: Relationship Between Big Data and Machine Learning

Since 2010, "Big Data" has become the universal term to refer to all the data generated by people from their mobile phones, social media, web history, and purchasing tendencies, plus any other information that organizations hold about them.

Why is big data unique from any other form of data? In one way, there is no difference; it is just zeros and ones at the end of the day. But the phrase "Big Data" is used to refer to a massive collection of different data which are volatile, and where an individual will struggle to categorize using traditional computer hardware and software.

It is also the fact that big data typically incorporates specific types of data that were not widely applied for customer analysis until relatively recently. In particular, big data involves:

Text. What people say and write can be processed to determine what they are talking about. If a product is being discussed positively or negatively, this is likely to indicate whether someone will buy the product or not.

Images: This deals with videos, photos, and medical imaging. One use of machine learning is to apply features in scans and x-rays to compute the chances that someone is suffering from a particular disease.

Social network data. This contains data about people's relationship and who they know. Network data includes the number and type of connections that people hold plus the data about connected individuals. If all members in your group are sci-fi geeks, that is probably a great indicator that you may be one too.

Biometrics: Data related to blood pressure, heartbeat, and so forth, gathered from smart watches, and so on.

The product generated: Everyday equipment from coffee makers to televisions are being developed to share information between themselves and over the internet. Nowadays, your washing machine, kettle, and so on can be controlled through your smartphone. The IoT concept is continuously being developed, but it will finally present lots of data that can be applied to refer to people's behavior using machine learning.

Back in the 1990s, there were no smart devices. Few people owned a mobile phone, and the internet was still in its developing stage. There was little electronic data about people. Supermarkets didn't have an idea of what individual customer purchased every week, insurance companies were not aware of how people drove, and the health services stored patient records in paper files.

The life of data science during these years was pretty simple because all the electronic data was stored up in a clean format of rows and columns. The data was also relatively static.

In the present world of big data, data is continuously being updated more frequently in real time. Additionally, most of it is "free form" unstructured data like speech, tweets, blogs, e-mails, and so on.

Another factor is that most of this data is often produced independently by the organization that wants to use itself, then they can control the way the information is formatted and apply checks and controls in place to make sure that the data is accurate and complete. However, if data is produced from external sources, there is no assurance that the information is correct.

Externally sourced data is always "messy." It demands a considerable amount of work to enhance it and get it to a useable format. Besides, there are a lot of concerns over the stability and on-going availability of the data, which generates a business risk in case it is an organization significant decision-making potential.

This means that traditional computer architectures that organizations use for things like processing sales transactions, managing customer account records, billing, and debt collection, are not best for storing and analyzing all of the new and different data types that are available. Similarly, over the last few years, an entire host of new and exciting hardware and software solutions have been created to deal with these new data types.

Notably, modern big data computer systems are excellent at:

Maintaining large data sets. Traditional databases have limits to the size of data they can hold at a reasonable cost. New methods of storing data have made it possible to store unlimited data.

Data cleaning and formatting. Different data needs to be transformed into a standard means before it can be applied for machine learning, report management, and other data related tasks.

It is processing data fast. Big data isn't just about the presence of more data. It has to be processed and analyzed quickly for it to be useful.

The problem with traditional computer systems is that practically they were too slow, cumbersome, and expensive.

New data processing and storage techniques like MapReduce/Hadoop have allowed tasks which would have consumed weeks or even months to process in just a few hours and at a fraction of the cost of more traditional data processing methods. The way Hadoop implements this is by letting data and data processing to spread across networks of cheap desktop PCS. Theoretically, thousands of PCs can be connected to generate massive computational potentials that are comparable to the largest supercomputers in existence.

Whether data is big or small, it doesn't have any intrinsic value. And one of the greatest mistakes that companies make is to assume that if they invest in big storage, and collect every data they can, then that will add value. Value can only be achieved if the data is processed and something useful is made from it.

ML is the primary tool that is used in data analysis and generating a predictive model about the behavior of people.

The best way to look at the link between ML and big data is that data is a raw material that is entered into a machine learning process. The tangible advantage to a business is determined from the predictive model that is generated at the end of the process, and not the data used to create it.

As a result, machine learning and big data are always discussed in the same breath, but there is no balanced relationship. You require machine learning to make the best out of big data, but you don't need big data to use machine learning effectively. If you have only a few items of information, then that is sufficient to start building predictive models and perform essential predictions.

How to Empower AI and Machine Learning through Big Data?

In the internet era, the amount of data is increasing across the world. This massive amount of information is processed via "Big Data Analysis." Alongside Big Data, the other two technologies that bring change to the IT world include AI and ML.

Nowadays, AI and ML are the forms of technologies that support computer systems and other connected devices in this way:

- Through recursive experiments
- Through a continuous update to data banks
- Through human interventions.

Machine learning and Artificial Intelligence are intertwined and peripherals motivated by the above technologies can be programmed in a manner that they can learn new things on their own using algorithms and programs. The machines can extract relevant and important information using big data analysis.

For instance, if a person has a leather garment company and wants to determine the market requirement of a country for a given season, then he can achieve this using Big Data Analytics. The information can be examined and accessed fast via reports that are produced using Big Data tools.

How Big Data Can Be Used to Extend AI and ML Workforce

As a result of AI, it is assumed that the complete workforce will be limited to a large extent in the coming years, and most of the tasks will be completed by AI-based computers. Still, big data can change this prediction. For Big Data analysis, human intelligence and sentiments are often required and applied, while machines don't have this human sentiments and emotions.

For this, let us consider the example of a Pharmaceutical Company that employs prominent data professionals to examine the data of the South-East Asian market. In this case, experts can rapidly since the pharmaceutical prescription of that place along with local reservations. Here, computer-focused big data analysis can never generate sensitive and contextual results.

In other words, the merging of Big Data, ML, and AI will only yield results for experts and capable data scientists. It will allow them to multiply in the market. Additionally, this merging will rise in the future by integrating three technologies.

How Can Big Data Benefit from AI and ML Service Providers?

At the moment, the international market of AI and ML solutions is incomplete. When Big Data is compiled with AI and ML machines, the devices become smarter, and their potential to implement complicated analysis increases. For that reason, complex AI solutions will cause the market and demand for these machines to increase.

In Latin America, big-data focused schools implement AI solutions for a long time. They are applying AI-based academic solutions and supporting a lot of educational institutes to implement AI into their educational systems. Thus, the educational market sector may experience significant growth because of this technological progress.

Big data assists in global diversification of AI and ML

With the rise of most innovative and advantageous technologies, the price of AI-based solutions and ML fall significantly. As a result, these AI-based techniques can be used by different religious, cultural, political affiliations, and spiritual inclinations. Additionally, AI and ML-based systems require to be trained based on local ethics.

Big Data analysis for different regions assists in designing the AI and ML-focused solutions depending on demographic requirements of that particular place without concentrating on their emotions. These solutions will be successful and famous for customers.

Business Areas Where Big Data, AI and ML Can Contribute

At the start, we said Big Data, AI, and ML can change business processes. Here are some of the familiar places that can be enhanced using these technologies.

- Improve the application of Social media data for business feed
- Enhance predictive models safer business using ML and AI support.
- Increase online Sale using chat bot analysis.

Overall, AI Big Data analytics, and ML can transform the business data so that it is accurate and straightforward. By extracting real-time business insights, decision-makers can implement strategic and better decisions. Volume and velocity aspects are the main factors that make Big Data powerful. In this case, we can say that both AI and Big Data complement each other. Business can receive real-world insights through the integration of Big Data and AI. But a lot of activity and companies are generating benefits from ML, AI, and Big Data integration.

In summary, ML, Big Data, and AI are the future of business across the world. If you want to assist your business to grow, then think about using these technologies. Where AI and ML deliver smarter and intelligent devices, Big Data may help in making decisions with more insights.

Chapter 11: How Machine Learning Can Enhance the Competitiveness of Any Business

Companies that are yet to make plans to invest and innovate will soon be eclipsed by the new economy driven by machine learning.

Machine learning is already transforming the whole world. As a major branch of AI, it allows computers to run and learn on their own, without any prior programming, by making use of data and experience instead of being explicitly programmed.

Netflix recommendations, YouTube recommendations, and virtual personal assistants like Alexa and Siri are some of the most popular AI applications. These features are not just for eCommerce and entertainment websites. Machine learning is now relevant to any organization and any size, for processes ranging from routine to revolutionary.

To stay competitive in the current market demands a working knowledge of artificial intelligence and machine learning skills.

Turning Data Overload into a Critical Mother Lode

Nowadays it is common that the more information you have, the better. This is especially true for business. The more information you have in your belt about your niche, products, customers, and marketplace, the higher your competitive advantage.

By 2017, 90 percent of data in the whole world has been generated in the last two years alone, at a rate of 2.5 quintillion bytes of data per day. Everything from mobile phones, web browsers, and sensors on devices provide an endless and exponentially growing stream of information. That is Big Data. However, not all that data is useful. The biggest hurdle for business lies in predicting which data is important, accurate, and actionable.

In The Evolution of Analytics by Patrick Hall, he says that organizations are now pushed to perform an advanced search in their data to identify new and innovative methods to increase efficiency and competitiveness.

The problem is that analyzing, gathering, and making use of all this data has grown past what is humanly possible, even applying traditional data analytics. This means companies are nearing a breaking point with the amount of data they can process, analyze, and implement.

Forrester Research approximates that about 60-73 percent of the data collected is never successfully used for strategic reasons.

The answer to transforming this massive data into something fit for construction lies in applying machine learning to automate the development of data analysis models. In general, humans can build 1-2 models per week, but machine learning can generate tens of thousands of models per week.

Machine learning not only deals with massive raw datasets, but it also craves for this data. The more you supply it with data, the smarter it becomes. Machine learning algorithms can define patterns, clusters, and associations among data, and then forecast results and recommend actions.

With the potential of machine learning and other applications of AI, your business can later make your data useful to business and your customers. In case data is not running your organization, it has to be.

Much of the information that companies have about their customers is self-reported data. In other words, this is data that is captured in lead forms from newsletter subscriptions, downloads, product registrations, customer service feedback, and surveys. The rest of the data is automatically monitored via website visits, search engine data, and cookies. Still, anonymous visitor data can be important. Social media is another data source, in particular reviews, engagements, and click-through. Data related to your competitors can be resourceful if you know how to mine it.

Most of the data generated by human beings are in text form. As a result, web crawling is a great way to mine information about what customers think. This then gives you an added advantage to stay ahead of competitors.

With a lot of the human-generated data being text. Web crawling is an important process for acquiring information about what customers are thinking for a competitive edge, maintaining brand reputation, and evaluating community awareness of organizational initiatives.

Transactional data is the most current, accurate, and used data. Some predict that by 2020, business transactions through the internet will hit 450 billion per day. Include the constant flow of data generated automatically via IoT like health monitors and appliances.

The size of data that we generate and copy annually will double each year and by 2020 is forecast to hit 44 zettabytes. Collecting and maintaining this data has grown past the potential of traditional storage. But Hadoop –an open source Java application has free modules that anyone can use. This application is mainly designed for extensive data sets. It has made it possible for the processing of large-scale data and is an important tool for competitive advantage.

Those who can successfully mine historical data can attain a significant advantage in the future. Alternatively, the cloud provides the opportunity for virtually unlimited storage at the lowest price point, and cloud leaders such as Microsoft Azure, Google Cloud, and Amazon Web Services are contributing unique and better computing services.

Those that push their IT architecture to the cloud have a better chance of staying ahead of the competition and building a system of interference that sets the stage of market leadership.

To optimize machine learning, diverse data is kept in a repository known as a "data lake." A data lake is different from traditional data warehouses because it stores the data in its raw, natural form, whether it is structured, unstructured, or semi-structured.

Although this makes the data easier to identify things, its level of inflexibility makes it hard to carry out innovative analyses.

A structured data makes it possible for you to respond to specific questions, but the structure may fail to accommodate issues that emerge at some point in the future.

The data lake idea permits unstructured data, and more flexibility to respond to new questions. Performing these analyses and responding entirely to further problems are accurate what machine learning performs, and hence provides the raw material for achieving a competitive advantage.

Now, you have the data with you, what next?

Ready with a large volume of data, machine learning algorithms can be "trained" depending on experience, then exposed to new data and released to hunt for patterns, learn from what they discover and create predictive models on their own.

We need to create programs that analyze not only a large volume of data to identify historical patterns but also intelligent enough to adapt to new data and upcoming patterns and examine the impact of a set of predictive frameworks.

The two widely adopted machine learning techniques for most businesses today require supervised learning and unsupervised learning.

1. When it comes to supervised learning, it depends on data that have labels like dates, names, and financial strings. Kept in relational databases, this data is common to businesses, but only makes 20 percent of all data. Structured data originates from human input, websites, or point of sale devices. Supervised learning algorithms are important when a specific output is known, or if you have a question you want to ask like determining new data points that match a certain target value. This is important for functions such as recommendation engines, predictive maintenance, and inventory control.

2. Unsupervised learning depends on data that is unstructured, has no historical labels, and doesn't fit well into a database. This kind of data includes customer transactions, document text, graphics, social media, and other content. Around 80-90 percent of the data in many organizations is unstructured. With unsupervised learning, the algorithm has to generate its inferences to identify what is searching for. It does this by looking for

clusters and hidden patterns. This kind of learning is important for market segmentation, hardware fault diagnostics, and fraud detection. The benefit of unsupervised learning is that it allows you to identify patterns in the data that you don't know.

Whether you apply supervised or unsupervised machine learning or a mix of the two, there are five ways that any business can take advantage of algorithms to establish a competitive advantage.

1. Automate business processes

Businesses can immediately incorporate machine learning to automate back-office processes. Most of these processes are high volume, rules-based functions that may operate on a "lights out" plan, freeing the time for employees to allow them to realize strategic company objectives.

Some of the simple functions consume 80 percent of total transactions being carried out by human workers. This increases the support costs adding no value to customers and the company itself.

Most companies are already outsourcing multiple mundane tasks to computers. By tracking the existing processes and learning to identify different instances, AI increases the number of invoices that can be automatically matched. This allows organizations to limit the amount of work delegated to service centers and allows the finance staff to concentrate on strategic tasks.

Lights-out-IT

In a survey conducted by Tata Consultancy Services in 2017, out of 835 companies surveyed, IT was the largest adopters of AI. It was not only used to monitor the moves of the hacker in the data center, but IT used AI to provide solutions to employees' tech support challenges, automate the task of putting new systems and ensure employees applied technology from certified vendors. About 34%-44% of companies surveyed were implementing AI in their IT departments.

Hands-off HR

Human resource and acquisition of skills are fields where AI can have a huge effect on limiting the workload, improving efficiency, and preventing bias. Chatbots plus other applications of machine learning can deal with repetitive HR tasks such as:

- Scheduling interviews, performing reviews, and other group meetings.

- Shortlisting job applicants from hundreds of resumes.

- Measuring and maintaining employee interactions.

- Respond to questions about company policies, office procedures, and basic conflict resolution.

- Polishing office workflows.

- Attracting and getting in touch with top talent.

A well-adopted machine learning technologies can save a lot of time through the application of predictive analysis to limit time wasting in hiring and making the process accurate and reliable.

Machine learning can still be used to enhance human productivity. For instance, auto-generating weekly reports and tracking hundreds of news items, social media mentions, and other information sources. These tools can be applied for monitoring data and predicting results, and helping corporate teams to prioritize product development and marketing efforts.

Ears-on analytics

Machine learning can extract data from brand new and massive sources of data that were never accessible via human means.

Other advanced uses of machine learning can make companies more competitive by building new products and changing the reliability of current ones.

The company IKEA-specialized in furniture development relies on a machine learning algorithm to review social media and find data to create new products that solve problems raised online.

Machine learning is also great at analyzing the huge volume of the historical sensor, failure data from devices, logistics, and machinery. The model's prediction may later recommend preventive maintenance, eliminate transportation, or even detect problems in real time that would show failure is imminent.

A lot of businesses have yet to discover the full potential of machine learning. The advantages extend far beyond faster supply chains and increased level of productivity.

2. Marketing

Even before the coming of the digital age, marketing professionals have been eager and early adopters of the rising technologies. Machine learning and AI are some of the popular tools for digital marketers. This evolution will take place and grow in the next few years as data grows, new models develop, and marketers build new strategies for getting the edge on their competition. AI offers the right answer to the ages-old advertising technique of finding the perfect message to the right individual at the correct time.

Machine learning can limit most of imprecise marketing nature. Applying behavioral data, marketers can focus their audiences in effective methods that highly enhance the chances of transforming shoppers to customers.

Here are some of the methods that companies apply in machine learning to improve their marketing and advertising, both offline and online.

- Customer churn risk modeling

- Demand prediction and sales projection.

- Targeted cross-sell and bundling.

- Dynamic and personalized product ranking.

- Augmented reality

- Polishing lead sourcing

- Micro-segmentation

- Optimized-message targeting

- Customer qualifying applying web data.

- Text-to-video creation.

Machine learning and other important technologies have created new methods for investing their market budget in smarter methods.

These technologies make it possible to check huge volumes of data in real time. Controlling big data and getting actionable insights are some of the most critical basics for any online business these days.

Smarter segmentation

List segmentation and personalization have been critical drivers since the time of direct mail. Most google natives enter a workforce where they pay-per-click, and the AI-marketing tools are ubiquitous to the point where they appear routine. This makes it difficult to differentiate from competitors. It demands expert knowledge of these skills and an open eye to new machine learning products and creative methods.

One thing that machine learning is important is the customer journey. Algorithms can tell what differentiates high-value customers from low-value ones, and so you know where to concentrate your sales efforts. Machine learning still identifies clusters of the best customers who share shocking properties. Your company may wish to review a section of customers that buy at the same time of the year and determine the factors that impact their purchasing behavior.

By mastering a certain cluster of customers, you can make decisions about the kind of products to suggest to customer groups via personalized offers and promotions.

Lead sourcing and scoring

For new leads, the traditional sourcing methods require purchasing lists or wasting hours looking for and scraping contract information from company sites.

Machines not only assist with the original data collection of lead generation, but AI can analyze unstructured data like phone calls, emails, and social posts to identify patterns and determine who is a right prospect.

The right marketing demands a deep understanding of customers and prospects. The more you thoroughly understand them, the more precisely you can concentrate on them. Not only machine learning automates this intelligence collection from familiar databases and sources, but the algorithms enter the external world to analyze, collect, predict and learn.

AI applications such as these are already present as products from third-party vendors; digital marketing experts don't need to be data scientists. But it is beneficial for marketers and executives to understand the key aspects of machine learning to master the potential and build strategies before making a massive investment in high-value resources. It is also important for marketers to learn the fields where humans do well and the things that are better left to computers.

Pay-per-click savings

If there is a field where machines do well, it is bidding. Bidding requires picking a human-defined strategy and changing bids based on the expected return on ad spend or cost per acquisition. Doing this manually or paying a third-party vendor to perform this can be expensive.

Since bidding depends on pattern recognition and statistics, this is one of the best application of machine learning. Machines can easily predict how a user may use an ad depending on previous behavior and the keyword stats.

Dynamic pricing

Another great application of AI for marketing lies in supporting elasticity in online pricing. Unlike human pricing models, AI-driven dynamic pricing can change at the time of shopping based on a broad range of real-time factors, including competitors pricing, shoppers level of interest, and prior interactions via previous marketing.

This demands a lot of data about how different customers are ready to pay for a great service change across different situations. But companies such as ride-share and airline services have successfully developed dynamic price optimization methods to improve revenue.

No matter how it is deployed in your marketing technology stack, machine learning eliminates waste-wasted budget, wasted labor, and so on. Machine learning can allow you to do more marketing with less capital. Search for opportunities where AI may assist you to generate more products with the same number of people you have today.

This is only the start of the bell curve for machine learning's role in marketing.

3. Transforming customer experience

One way that machine learning can assist any business strike a competitive advantage is via applications that analyze and enhance the overall customer experience.

In a connected economy, customers expect highly personalize and real-time interactions. Nowadays, nearly every company tries to remain competitive by enhancing their digital experiences with customers and tapping data and insights to make those experiences important and valuable.

Churn modeling

There are different methods that machine learning can set this difference to your customers. First is to help you understand them. Churn modeling is good not only for marketing but also for customer support and product enhancement.

Machine learning allows big data analysis at speeds that aren't humanly possible. Algorithms can be applied in determining these factors like customer purchasing behavior, marketing histories, and website. Next, they can determine the risk models that compare simulations based on preventive actions to find out how these interventions affect the odds of churning. Risk analysis from churn modeling can provide live customer support teams with the best problem resolution paths.

Customer support

In a 2017 study published in Chatbots Magazine highlighted that about 55% of UK consumers report that the most critical factor when it comes to the customer experience is finding a prompt and effective response to questions.

Companies require to generate faster customer service replies, and all the data associated with the customer journey, previous interactions, and other issues. Machine learning makes this a reality.

Thanks to the low-cost speech analytic tools and recording, tracking customer service interactions among themselves can also provide insights to contact centers.

Rather than just directing callers via prompts, speech analytics will assist classify them and review the responses based on what you say and how you say it.

Chatbots

Automated customer support via AI-driven Chatbots is already achieving acceptance and popularity. Since 75% of all consumers fall between 18-25, intelligent digital agents are the solution for providing customers with quick web chat service.

Additionally, because of the thousands of AI-based customer support, consumers can now comfortably interact with Chatbots.

Consumers are used to interacting with technology via voice commands smart assistants, smart devices, and automated call centers. Machine learning supports speech-enabled Chatbots to improve customer service inquiries if relevant.

According to a 2018 McKinsey Global Institute report, deep learning analysis of audio makes it possible for systems to review customer's emotional tone, in case the customer responds badly to the system, the call can be rerouted automatically to human managers and operators.

Social media monitoring

Optimizing the power of machine learning to track social media is a great move for companies to remain competitive. Including social media gossip when mixing it with data from other transactions and customer demographic enhances product marketing and can still boost individualist product recommendations.

According to the McKinsey report, "Next product to buy" recommendations that focus on individual customers can result in a twofold rise in the rate of sales conversions.

Social media monitoring still makes an important step in ensuring the presence of quality customer support.

With the development of global chatter on sites like Facebook and Twitter, it can be hard for even a big business to attain all this valuable feedback.

Machine learning integrated with linguistic algorithms improves the process of establishing what customers say about you almost anywhere.

Social media monitoring is a great way to apply AI to collect competitive advantage. The same way you can monitor the mention of your company, the same concept can be applied to gain market share from your competitors.

Customer loyalty is diminishing because of other options, especially when these alternative options poach someone.

Becoming one with the machines

Applying a "wait and see" approach using machine learning is not an option, specifically for companies in competitive sectors.

But turning a blind eye on competitors who have robots is not an issue for B3C. All companies face challenges in the technology curve.

Early evidence shows that there is a business case to be achieved, and that AI can generate value to companies ready to apply it across operations and within their core functions.

Also, early AI adopters that integrate strong digital capability with proactive plans attain a higher profit margin and expect the performance gap with other firms to increase in the next few years.

Besides that, the cold start challenge with AI is a big challenge for many companies, whether big or small. The rapid changes in technology have made a lot of companies to become clueless about what they need to concentrate.

Most businesses are already convinced of the business example for machine learning. Based on a 2017 report highlighted by Louis Columbus in Forbes, 84 percent of the executive's report that AI allowed them to stay ahead of their competitors.

If you are starting the strategy phase of integrating machine learning into your competitive toolkit, you have several options. Some experts consider machine learning to represent the next phase in the evolution of analytics. Consulting with professional data scientists is an important first step. But for certain companies that may not be an option.

Most companies are establishing links with universities to identify recent graduates from specialized advanced degree programs in data and analytics.

But to some level, most organizations must implement the talent they already have.

Upgrading your staff in AI and machine learning technologies is a smart move.

For new companies in AI, beginning from inside is a safer investment. A common mistake is hiring several machine learning professionals who are too expensive before getting the data infrastructure and data accessibility in their organizations in order.

That is something that is usually a big problem, and what finally happens is a low return on investment, which results in bad engineering.

A certain report published by Gartner says that by 2022-one in five workers doing nonroutine tasks will depend on AI to perform the job. Well, this is not bad news for workers.

Often, we have realized that automating fairly simple transactions and workflows may let employees and customers spend a lot of time elsewhere, leading to a lot of value at the end.

Organizations that concentrate only on automation will transform their competitive edge. The most successful will concentrate on skills that distinguish them, and that can't be duplicated by AI or ML.

Those skills can be summarized up in a single word: humanness.

Is applying ML worth the pains? Experts say yes because ML offers the tools for visibility into your organization, processes, products, customers and even competitors.

Instant access to on-demand insights provides business with the edge they require to survive in a competitive environment.

Chapter 12: The Future of AI

While organizations and people struggle to control a wide range of information and a growing range of devices, there are still a few new techniques to apply to make a quality decision based on AI and the IoT.

It's around 10 am on a Tuesday and Jane, a marketing specialist is working with her colleagues to compile a presentation for a new business pitch. The client is a big corporate company, and the pressure is on to get the account.

Networking with teams in other locations, Jane has data coming in by text, e-mail, WhatsApp and instant messaging and by phone. At the same time, she is looking online for important facts and data for her project.

The global population is expected to hit 7.6 billion in 2020 with the number of IoT connected devices expected to increase between 20-30 billion by the same year. How can Jane and hundreds of million others control these information sources, determine what is important, and make the correct decision?

Compute this growing number of people and devices, and you will begin to see an exponential rise of data and ubiquitous information that is already generating 'infoxication.'

Artificial intelligence seems to solve this issue by building a set of technologies that can assist control information, and look for reliable data sources, accept informed decisions and take advantage of improved cognition.

Workplace hub focuses on the office, and in particular, the workplace of the future. It integrates all of an organization's technology through a single centralized platform plus enhancing efficiency by decreasing the general costs of IT management and service provision.

It offers real-time, data-driven insights that transform business processes. By implementing AI and IoT systems, workplace hub will change in the next five years to become what the company refers to as a cognitive hub.

This new technology will use intelligent edge computing to AI and augment human intelligence to expand the network of human interfaces and improve collaboration between teams and individuals.

Cognitive Hub will become a great platform for a company's information flows within the digital sector and offer augmented intelligence-based on the kind of services that everyone can apply.

It will also connect future devices like augmented reality glasses, flexible screens, and smart-walls. Cognitive hub merges entire company wisdom using AI to collect and process data to make life simple for teams, individuals, and companies, enabling them to work efficiently.

Although some people think that cloud computing is going to diminish, the fact is that it won't die. Instead, it will diverge and transform into a cortex-like structure made of complex three-dimensional tree. In this modern age, cloud computing is the glue between intelligent automation, cognitive computing, and other fields related to AI.

There is still a lot of work to deliver in the cognitive hub, but workplace hub has already transformed the way we work by allowing us to control the rapid rise in devices, connections, and information.

The future of AI in 2020

Talking of Millenials and the next coming generation, what distinguishes us from our predecessors is the discoveries, humans have so far invented and developed almost everything that we can touch in virtual. The only common thing between us, predecessors and the coming generation is the brain that changes the way we communicate and how we view things. Artificial Intelligence had been predicted for years, but it was initially connected to robots only. But now AI is integrated into almost everything we use and consider smart. AI is a software that emulates humans or has human-like behavior.

It has always been predicted, seen and witnessed as something with excellent ability to make us sit at a comfortable place enjoying while some of the tasks are completed, saving our time and consuming minimum energies and efforts to get things done.

Programming

This brings us to a new world where you can complete different things you never thought you could complete. AI connects us and acts as a transition between discrete actions. In other words, it allows you to interact in multiple things at one time, like translating from one language to another instantly. Ever since computers were introduced, we have been relying on a set of rules for dealing with our actions and letting us customize from their setting page. Transferring the same technology into AI requires the absence of these rules and training the algorithm of the computer to link up with the actions.

Predictions 2019

Artificial intelligence provides us with variables to work with and allows us to process all the variables in a programmatic style, which is simpler and provides a transparent level of confidence. It emerges as a controversial, but predicting what is going to take place in the coming years is accurate if done within the scientific realm of statistics. From the start, computers were known for dealing with all the mathematical tasks. Computing statistical relevance which is the cornerstone of machine learning when it comes to diagnosing diseases, predicting weather patterns, and playing chess. Since we are always heading towards increased data volume, and processing power, that makes the computer suitable.

Decisions

These days, companies make decisions based on the data extracted from management information systems because that data directly emerges from operations of their company-making it crucial to break or make rules. Integrating AI and decision management technologies are sufficient to push decision-making to different levels. Proficiencies in AI also benefit decision management technologies when it comes to defining customer data into prognostic models of important trends. This new trend has already made other departments such as marketing and consumer to change their efforts based on the major demographic.

We can say it is a matured technology with digital banking, which is currently being used in different enterprise applications.

Interactions

AI generates new forms of the interface using the least effort. With the invention of mouse and keyboards in our lives, we are using computers every day and conveniently as time goes. For digital communications, we have learned how to program and code so we can realize better results. Now, as the codes can be converted into human sentences and interrupt input from sensors and cameras-this interaction can be conducted smoothly and naturally.

What you should expect with the future of AI technology

Different types of technological inventions are changing the way we live, how we interact and move on with our everyday lives, but AI may provide the most interesting changes. Although AI has been around for quite some time, the recent changes have made AI adaptable. Reviewing the future of AI, one can see a world where AI controls each aspect of our lives.

The most promising AI innovations

Overall, artificial intelligence will change every phase of our everyday life. Although we shall find for ways to incorporate it at home, AI will still be used by companies, businesses, and government.

Right now we have self-driving cars that have been introduced on the road. While the self-driving industry is expected to expand in the coming years, the U.S transport department is already creating policies and regulations to control AI-driven vehicles.

Currently, the self-driving vehicles are in the lowest category where the vehicles require a human driver. Despite this, the ultimate plan is to create a complete automated self-driving car, which is predicted to be effective and safe. The public transportation sector and firms are still concentrating on AI to develop self-driving bus and planes.

AI and Robotics will integrate

Cybernetics has already incorporated AI, and that is a progress that is bound to continue. By adding AI technology into robotics, soon we shall improve our bodies, providing us with endurance, longevity, and strength. Although cybernetics may make us improve our bodies, the use of this technology is focused on assisting the disabled. Individuals with permanent paralysis or amputated limbs can be provided with a better life.

AI will create complete functional robots

Besides allowing us to improve our bodies, AI technology is predicted to help us build artificial lifeforms. Science fiction has, for a long time, exploring the idea of human-like robots capable of performing complex interactions. As the field of robotics continues to change and include AI, robots will become important in different ways. For example, they can pick a dangerous task and do work that may be hazardous to our health.

Impact on humans

Based on some statistics released by Gartner, by 2012, AI will eradicate 1.8 million jobs and replace it with 2.3 million jobs. If you consider the journey of human beings from the past three industrial revolutions toward the present digital revolution, our lives and standard of workings have changed substantially, and they would be changed again. Consider the world where we talk about work-life balance by spending two days working. It is pretty much expected.

But with these synthetic substances, AI is a massive deal. At the moment, we are in reality because we know where things finish fast, with more exactness, and in light of better learning.

2020 will be a great year in AI business progression because automated reasoning will resort to positive employment spark.

With the arrival of 2020, AI-based jobs will hit two million net-new employments in 2025.

Different advancements in the past have been linked with a short-lived employment misfortune, monitored by recuperation, at that point, the business will change, and AI will probably take this course. AI will improve the profitability of multiple occupations, disposing of a large number of center and low-level positions.

The future of AI in the workplace

Smart devices aren't just transforming our homes, but they are finding their way into multiple industries and disrupting the workplace. AI can change productivity, efficiency, and accuracy across a company.

However, many people fear that the advancement of AI will cause machines and robots to replace human workers and look at this development in technology as a threat instead of a tool to change our lives.

With discussion of AI going on in 2019, businesses require to understand that self-learning and black-box potential are not the answer. Many organizations have started to experience the unlimited power of AI, using the benefits of AI to improve human intelligence and acquire real value from their data.

Since there is a lot of evidence that shows the advantages of intelligent systems, many decision-makers have started to grasp the potential of AI. Research done by EY shows that organizations incorporating AI at the enterprise level are improving operational efficiency and making informed decisions.

The first companies to implement AI achieves competitive advantage. That is because it can reduce the cost of operations, and other head counts. From a business perspective, this is a positive thing, but not for people working in jobs that can be taken over by machines. Of course, the introduction of AI will create some conflict between humans and machines.

As we continue to build innovative systems, AI will have a huge impact on our economy by creating jobs that demand a specific skill.

There is a probability that AI will come to replace certain jobs that involve repetitive tasks and eclipse the current human ability. AI technologies will decide the place of humans.

Automated decisions will be responsible for tasks such as loan approval, detecting corruption, and financial crime.

Organizations will experience a rise in production levels because of the progress in automation.

How to maximize AI

Since many jobs may be affected by the development of AI, it is good to look at some of the problems that AI may bring.

- The business should find a solution to the bias problem around AI by identifying an effective implementation.

- The government must make sure that the profits of AI are shared in the society between the ones affected and those not affected by the developments.

To effectively take advantage of AI, problems must be addressed at an educational level. Education systems can focus on empowering students in tasks linked to working with AI.

This demands a lot of emphases be applied to STEM subjects. Besides, subjects that improve creativity and emotional abilities should be encouraged. While artificial intelligence will be productive than human beings, humans will always do better than computers in jobs that require imagination and relationship building.

Artificial intelligence will transform the world both inside and outside the workplace. Instead of concentrating on the fear of around automation, businesses require to embrace technologies to make sure they implement the most effective AI systems to improve and complement human intelligence.

Ensuring that the machines don't take over

When Stephen Hawking cautioned about the possibility of a certain technology, then it makes sense to think about it.

Stephen Hawking said in 2014 that AI could lead to the end of the human race. There many possible benefits because everything provided by civilization is a product of human intelligence. It is hard to predict what we may attain when this intelligence is reflected by the tools AI may offer, but the elimination of disease and poverty cannot be undermined.

Humanity's potential death at the hands of machines is a long journey. In a PWC's March 2017 economic report, it predicts that by 2030 close to 30 percent of UK jobs could be taken over by machines. Workers in the storage, manufacturing, transportation, and retail sectors are the ones to be at risk.

Despite this chilling report by PWC, some people hold a different believe than this. For example, Accenture forecasts that AI technologies will generate an additional $814billion to the UK economy.

There have been a lot of fearful stories about AI, and several studies have concentrated heavily on the job displacement effect. However, some people think this as a simplistic view.

The traditional boosters of economic growth and labor no longer work to increase the GDP, but AI provides hope.

The argument is that AI, to the point that it can be a new form of virtual labor, can effectively become a new wave of production that can transform the general picture of growth.

AI will support both intelligent automation and augmentation. Intelligent automation is different from the automation we had seen some time ago. It involves the application of data to deliver services and intelligently implement tasks. There is still a large effect of augmentation. Taking the things, we already do and allowing us to perform them productively.

What has awakened AI in the business industry is the increasing cost of computer power and an increase in cloud availability. The cloud-based platform, which relies on AI to analyze the shape of the network of data in near-real time, is applied by companies and governments across the world.

You can store each bit of data you find and combine the data with these algorithms to create an opportunity where it did not exist before.

If you require a professor specialized in mathematics to help you out with interpretation of AI and ML algorithms, then you cannot persuade your senior executives to proceed.

Ayasdi has achieved this by developing applications that rely on the underlying technology but focused at certain business challenges like helping hospitals determine the best practice in healthcare from their data so that they can generate the best quality care at a lower price.

Providers of AI are already helping firms and organizations to become smarter and efficient. There is a huge economic potential from AI technologies, but how can you develop people and infrastructure so that we get the economic benefit.

Jobs might be different in the coming years-you could be working alongside a robot or teaching them. How can you educate people now so that they are fit to deal with that?

Things to note about the future of AI

1. **AI is growing faster than you think and expanding exponentially.**

2. **You use artificial intelligence every day**

Google Now, Cortana, and Siri are some of the common examples of AI, but AI is definitely around us. It can be found in cars, video games, vacuum cleaners, and lawnmowers. E-commerce software, international financial markets, and medical research are some of the many examples.

3. **Robots will take over part of your job**

You could be doing well in your job, but the task you do may already be automatable, or it will soon be automated. How soon? In the next 30 years, most jobs will be done by robots, that is according to professor Moshe Vardi of Rice University. That may look bad, but many researchers in the field believe that technological unemployment will create the door to a future where work is something where people do as pleasure, but not out of necessity.

4. Many intelligent people believe building AI to human level is a risky thing to do.

Once machines become smart like human beings, so many worrying things can take place. There is a minimal probability that development in AI will stop at this point.

5. If AI gets smarter than us, then we have little chance of learning it.

We will never understand the things a super intelligent device can do, even if it attempts to describe to us. It may attempt for years to train us the simplest things it knows, but the actions would useless.

6. There three methods that super intelligent AI could work

7. AI could be the reason why we have never met aliens

An Intelligent future

The high power of modern computing technology plus the rise of human-like robots would make you understand that intelligent machines are not far from taking over our jobs.

However, the reality is that AI programs are sometimes suitable than humans at certain tasks, like playing video games and pattern recognition. They are still far from realizing the type of general intelligence that humans possess.

The human brains took years to grow its complex and efficient functions, and despite the ability of computers, they are not likely to suit their abilities for decades.

There is still a lot that even simple animal brains can show us how information is processed. For example, animals like bees and octopus reveal a certain level of intelligence despite lacking a forebrain.

These animals can perform better than AI based on how fast they can master different tasks with little time. Essentially, deep learning network requires millions of samples before they can learn.

In summary, artificial intelligence has been buzzing in our ears by almost all professions. Take, for instance, 2018, A.I has grown more than ever anticipated. Today, people have started to acknowledge AI after discovering how much it is going to make their lives peaceful. The general advantage of A.I is that it generates choices and activities of humans minus the natural human insufficiencies, for a sensation and time limitation.

Chapter 13: Global Tech Companies Compete in AI

When people think of AI, some switch their minds to methods they can apply to save the human race from rogue machines; familiar story performed on Hollywood screens in the past decades.

Although machine intelligence is far from coming close to human consciousness, an AI conflict is taking place in real life, and this is not between robots and humans, but among businesses competing to take over a lucrative market.

The history of AI date back to 1950, a time when computer science pioneer Alan Turing wrote and published a paper mentioning that one-day machines will think like humans.

Between Turing's landmark paper published several years ago and today's wild market valuations, significant AI developments have either fallen in terms of research or involved machines defeating people at human games.

IBM won the pride when its Deep Blue computer overcame chess grandmaster Garry Kasparov. After 15 years, Watson defeated human beings on TV game show Jeopardy. Not long, Google captured the headlines with the 2015 victory of the AlphaGo program.

AI today

In the last couple of years, AI has made huge strides beyond research and televised fights between man and machine to become a technology loved and used by millions of people daily. Thanks to a trio of essential developments.

First, the ubiquitous application of online services, smart devices, and social media has made data to become available on a mass scale. Data is the power for building algorithms for deep learning, a form of AI that makes it possible for machines to learn and create software. The more data that the system receives, the better it becomes at completing tasks.

Hosting large amounts of data was previously an expensive initiative that would have continued to prevent AI development had it not been for the coming of affordable cloud storage from Google, Microsoft, and Amazon.

Completing this was the rise of powerful chipsets, boosting the process for training computers to behave and act like humans.

All this reflects the great promise of AI can finally be attained in industries extending from healthcare and energy to self-driving cars. The result is a competition among the most significant technology firms to cement their position as leaders in AI applications.

The AI market

The importance of the AI industry can now be experienced not only in the realms of enterprises starting to implement this technology but also in the market performance of companies that are already enjoying the demand.

American chip creator Nvidia, for instance, has seen its stock price increase in the past year after the graphics processing components became the favorite choice for companies training AI systems. This motivated rival Intel to spend around $15.3 billion to buy Mobileye, a chip creator for trucks and cars.

Some years ago, Nvidia committed itself as a company for investing in deep learning. Now that commitment is generating a lot of fruits, and we find ourselves in a state of leadership because this new computing model takes the world by storm.

Data dominance

Ownership of data is vital because tech giants cannot hold all of the world's AI talent, but they can own the data required to train AI. This has led to a big six of tech firms said to enhance AI because of the data-intensive nature of their primary businesses.

Google, Apple, Amazon, and Microsoft, for instance, have managed to take advantage of the data they have gathered from their other businesses to grab an early lead in the race for intelligent personal assistants. Facebook has relied on machine-learning to build a messenger chatbot, while IBM has been an early driver in the cognitive computing sector with Watson. All have made their AI technology open to allow any developer to create on their cloud infrastructure because they know data is the main difference.

If AI truly emulates human consciousness, the stuff of films in our lifetime will originate from one of those companies because they are the only ones with the data to train a model of that complexity.

AI will trigger a new data gold rush, defined by data-driven acquisitions. Companies that search data assets around a specific use-case will win. The final barrier to entry will be unimaginable.

This ability to lead in specific use-cases implies that non-tech firms have the chance to get a piece of their segment. Engineering giants are investing heavily in factory automation.

Similarly, there is a notion that AI startups and companies in other industries can gain from the democratization of AI via the big six's open source tools like Microsoft's CNTL.

Some consider this democratization as necessary in making sure AI can solve the broad level of business and societal challenges, and that restricting innovation to a small pool of companies will provide them with a lot of control and destroy AI's ability.

This has sent chills because Google's largest reservoir of data has some weak points. If Google and Amazon dictate the world of AI, then the resulting systems will be biased, even if they have the best objectives and intentions.

The more people take part in AI debates, the more industries will gain, and the earlier we shall see the effects across the business, government, and society.

However, some people think that the option to democratize AI is gone. Spreading innovation past the big six is unrealistic because of the absence of programming talent and high costs of acquiring it.

Even with the presence of free platforms, you still require to have an experienced, and specialized data scientist to develop efficient solutions that offer real value to users.

When an extensive AI programming skill is finally brought to the market, the big six companies don't have to worry. By making their AI technology open source, they have already sent a message to the rest of the world that software is no longer an advantage to them, but data is.

Despite AI being present in people's homes and many other big businesses, the most powerful applications are yet to be achieved. But when they do arrive, the big six companies have set the path to benefit the most, but still, they have each other to compete with. At the same time, the market will be sufficient enough for startups and enterprises to build a lead using special use-cases.

Chapter 14: Building an Enterprise AI Strategy

Overwhelmed by a decade-long run that has realized considerable gains in computer power and storage costs, businesses have the relevant requirements to ensure intelligence is a reality.

The question enterprises need to address today is not whether to become intelligent, but is a matter of how and how fast. Every business will become knowledgeable in the same manner every enterprise is a digital enterprise. If they don't evolve and embrace AI, then they will stop to exist.

To realize intelligence, enterprises require to adapt and develop an intelligent application approach while simultaneously preparing the organization to narrow that intelligence. A strategy created around smart applications enables enterprises to develop experience, express business value, and establish a framework for repeatability.

The focus, however, is to create intelligent applications. The ability to identify patterns in data without preconceived notions: this depends heavily on unsupervised machine-learning techniques.

An unsupervised technique automatically chooses algorithms and dramatically limits risks by removing bias. The ability to accurately predict relies on new data models trained on historical data. This is a standard measure for many ML algorithms but is always confused for the whole field.

Intelligent applications must learn to justify their assertions. Black-box models cannot complete mission-critical tasks if they cannot be interpreted to the business owner. Transparency and justification generate trust.

Unexplored intelligence must also be accompanied by action. This means intelligence must train other applications autonomously or fall in the subject matter experts' workflow.

Lastly, intelligent applications are built with the ability to detect and react as data changes. An intelligent system is one that continuously learns.

By developing intelligent applications that involve all these properties, enterprises have a place to start. To narrow that effort, it requires extra considerations involving technology strategy and organizational changes.

For instance, organizations will always conduct a small-scale experiment using a subset of the above components. This builds a false sense of security for most enterprises. Wins implemented against sterile data or in an operational vacuum are not likely to convert well when required to scale to real-world scenarios such as detecting cyber-criminals within billions of financial transactions, or monitoring and eliminating global health epidemics. Establishing real-world applications will prepare an enterprise for long-term success.

This commitment to deployable intelligence should not come at the cost of speed. Enterprises that set fast timelines tend to learn pretty faster.

Intelligent systems will transform how you conduct specific business processes. Understanding this fact, ahead of time will allow the enterprise to optimize on the knowledge and to consolidate the wins, thereby establishing momentum for the future applications of intelligence. At the center of a successful change lies a center of excellence. From here, best practices are developed, processes change is improved, and prioritization is established depending on operational readiness, business need, and other factors.

The next generation of leaders will emerge from this center of excellence. So you need to staff it adequately.

Each organization should customize its intelligence approach to specific business needs. In the future, every analytics company will change to become an AI company. These changes will make it hard to differentiate truth from fiction, but the features defined to identify, justify, predict, and learn should present a framework to examine the validity. That framework, integrated with an application-first approach, should allow organizations to overcome these transformational changes.

Artificial Intelligence has the ability to change every business in the same manner the internet has completely changed the way we conduct our business. From smarter services and products tailored for business processes, AI has the potential to change everything. Those businesses that don't take advantage on the transformative power of AI risk being left behind.

That is the reason why you need develop an AI strategy for your enterprise whether small or big. To get the most out of AI, it has to be related to your business strategy and your entire picture of strategic goals. So the first step in any AI strategy is analysis of your business strategy. After all, you don't want to miss this strategy and apply AI to an irrelevant business objective.

In this stage, you need to ask yourself whether your business strategy is right? Is your strategy still current in the world of smarter services and products?

Conclusion

AI is the driving force of new enterprises. The main assumption made is that human intelligence can be represented using symbolic structures and operations.

A huge debate exists on whether AI can be a mind, or imitate the human mind, but no need to wait for the results of this debate, nor the hypothetical computer that can model the whole human intelligence.

AI is poised to make a vast transformational change on business. Informational technology is no longer about the automation process and programming business logic, but insight is the new currency, and the rate at which it can scale that insight and the knowledge it generates is the foundation of value creation and the goal of competitive advantage.

The effects of AI will increase in the coming decade, as every industry will change its main processes and business models to take advantage of AI and ML. The problem now lies in business management, implementation, and imagination. For business leaders, it is crucial to devise a plan for incorporating AI work in the organization.

AI demands that you have the vision to fulfill. But your vision should not be a cookie cutter, and so your AI application should not be either. With the advice and discussion in this book, you can move forward to introduce advanced analytics into your company strategy and understand the pros and cons of different methods depending on your goals.

Fields such as manufacturing, sports, banking, and retail have already found applications for machine learning and AI.

Don't forget that the current machines can complete narrowly defined tasks with great accuracy, and that accuracy is only as good as the quantity of the data that powers the model. The current state of ML will, with the input of customized data, attain countless improvements to existing products, and finally, lead to the development of free-standing AI.

However, as machine learning gets complex, we will move towards a sophisticated AI. The complexity of AI is realized through neural networks. That said, we hope you have enjoyed reading this book, found it resourceful.

www.ingramcontent.com/pod-product-compliance
Lightning Source LLC
Chambersburg PA
CBHW071200050326
40689CB00011B/2199